ADVANCE PRAISE

"Finally, a framework and processes for how to treat employees equally and engage them intentionally to create meaningful experience while adding value to their career journey. A requirement for employee engagement, attraction, retention, and development leaders. A must-read!"

—REGINALD BEAN, VICE PRESIDENT OF CULTURE
AND ENGAGEMENT AT COCA-COLA

"Donte and his team did for us what we had not been able to do on our own: repair a broken dynamic in leadership that was trickling down through our organization."

—MIKE STROMMEN, CEO OF PROCESS DISPLAYS (PD INSTORE)

"Adherence to stated cultural aspirations starts with leaders who demonstrate by example. Gimmicks, gaming of surveys, and other tactics are quickly sniffed out by teammates. Living this out takes humble, transparent, honest leadership at all levels. Donte and Randall are vanguards to making culture aspirations attainable."

—BOBBY HARRIS, COO OF INSTINCT PET FOODS

"*Part business development, part personal development, From CULTURE to CULTURE shows how organizational leaders can implement real cultural integrity, connecting company values to leadership behaviors and to the employee experience. And you can scale it across the enterprise! How innovative yet simple.*"

—ALEXANDRA KERR, COO OF GEHL FOODS

"*I have worked with Randall and his team, and they helped us significantly improve by focusing on the right leadership skills and behaviors that optimize performance and people. Highly recommend!*"

—BILL SCHREIBER, CEO OF O-AT-KA

"*Excellence is a journey, not a destination. There are always opportunities for improvement, and the journey must be continuous in nature. The key is to have a sound systematic approach toward fact-based cycles of improvement—that is, a definitive process around clearly understanding the current state and the required improvements to deliver on this desired state. Randall and the Powers team have created a cultural performance management process design to do just that: Define the current state; define the desired state; and define the systematic approach, deployment plan, and measurement system to take the organization on the journey of cultural excellence.*"

—PETER BROWN, CEO OF SEABOARD

"*Randall and his team have helped us significantly with cultural and operational improvement by focusing on the right leadership skills and behaviors that optimize performance and people. Highly recommend!*"

—CHRIS CARTER, SVP OF OPERATIONS AT FOSTER FARMS

"*I am fortunate to have had leaders early in my career who recognized the power of linking values, people, experience, and continuous improvement to unlock the potential of an organization. This book is a must-read primer for all leaders wishing to truly develop their teams at all levels plus accelerate and mature the cultural values we say we have and measure them in real time—incredible!"*

—JIM ERICKSON, VP-GM OF OPERATIONS AT CHROMALLOY

"Our culture has always had a strong set of family values. From CULTURE to CULTURE shows how to teach our leaders to connect these values to leadership behaviors and to the employee experience. Innovative, simple, and scalable across the organization."

—DAN HUBER, CEO OF FOSTER FARMS

"Every organization has a culture. It never happens by accident, but it may or may not be the one that they want. KPIs are important company staples, but the understanding and application of CPM to ensure alignment of values, definitions, and behaviors is how you move exponentially toward your desired state. Randall and Donte brilliantly and directly break the myths around culture and deliver practical advice on how to think about this critical enabler of success."

—VICTOR DAVIS, SENIOR DIRECTOR OF BEYOND MEAT

"Randall, Donte, and their team partnered with us to facilitate our team through the process of developing and implementing the knowledge and skills on how to better optimize our cultural and operational performance. They helped us by focusing on the right leadership skills and behaviors that optimize performance and people, right at the point of execution. Highly recommended!"

—SHANNON DEARY-BELL, CEO OF NOR-CAL BEVERAGE

"I have worked with Randall and his team, and they helped us significantly improve by focusing on the right leadership skills and behaviors that drive real performance, connectivity, and accountability from the corner office to the shop floor. Highly recommended!"

—CHRIS HAMILTON, CEO OF RED COLLAR

FROM CULTURE TO CULTURE

from

CULTURE

to

CULTURE

THE SYSTEM TO DEFINE, IMPLEMENT, MEASURE,
AND IMPROVE YOUR COMPANY CULTURE

DR. DONTE VAUGHN
& RANDALL POWERS

LIONCREST
PUBLISHING

FROM CULTURE TO CULTURE
The System to Define, Implement, Measure, and
Improve Your Company Culture

ISBN   978-1-5445-2614-0   *Hardcover*
         978-1-5445-2612-6   *Paperback*
         978-1-5445-2613-3   *Ebook*
         978-1-5445-2615-7   *Audiobook*

Dr. Donte Vaughn:

For my wife, Hazel, and son, Dylan, who inspire me daily to pursue my earthly purpose from God. I love you more than I could ever accurately express and am grateful to fulfill our family's role of husband, father, and leader.

For the individuals I work with every day, thank you for entrusting me with your personal and professional leadership development. I become a better me because of you.

Randall Powers:

To my wife, Beth, this book is affectionately dedicated. You have walked hand in hand with me through this long journey from seeing the problem, struggling to formulate the solution, to that time of illumination years later when the answer was revealed to me in a moment of clarity in the bright sunshine. You have listened patiently, tolerated my struggling moments, and even playfully partnered with me in the progress of the development of this solution. I am forever grateful. I am forever committed. I am forever in love with you.

CONTENTS

LET'S GET REAL

Face it. Many believe money makes the world go round, and most business executives make decisions based on their bottom line. It's their job.

Driving increased engagement between leaders and their team members, at all levels of the organization, is a must for any successful company. Therefore, your organization must adopt an effective strategy to measure and improve how employees are engaged to ensure desired performance outcomes are realized. Many strategies have been applied, few have succeeded in the short term, and even fewer in perpetuity.

The answer lies in the "C" word.

Yes, the unspeakable word that makes people do a double-take when they hear it. Especially in a professional setting. That's right; we're referring to culture. Specifically, company culture.

Company Culture: *The values we share, the language we use, the behaviors we display, and the connections we have with others. The values set the standard for how individuals must engage and interact. The definition of the values determines the behaviors individuals must exhibit within a company culture. The shared understanding of the definition of these values and behaviors establishes the common language used within a company culture. The practice of these behaviors establishes how individuals engage and interact within a company culture.*

However, the reality is many of these executives rarely associate their company culture with their bottom line. You'd be hard-pressed to find a midsized organization with a large annual budget for "company culture." For the majority of businesses, investments in initiatives to "improve" company culture have not been deemed a priority. This reality is rooted in a deep history—stemming as far back as the 1980s, when company culture (previously known as "corporate culture") was presented as nothing more than a theoretical ideal-state to address how stakeholders collaborated or interacted with one another. It was used to foster innovation during a time when companies like IBM and Kodak were at the top of their game!

Why?

Because they adopted technological innovations in the wake of the market potential wave realized by leveraging computer technology. During this time—across a landscape of polka-dot socks, baggy jeans, and big hair—business leaders coined the phrase "corporate culture" to address the comradery and creativity many perceived as necessary to be innovative.

In the early 1980s, "corporate culture" was first introduced by organizational theorist Linda Smircich. However, the primary focus of company culture was on the benefits for internal stakeholders. Since, this has been the focus for most business leaders. Until now, many of them asked two primary questions when considering the efficacy of their company culture:

1. How does our company culture influence frontline leaders' engagement with their employees?
2. Does that engagement enhance productivity and increase profitability?

This focus on internal stakeholders remains pertinent to the "culture" conversation today; as most business leaders would agree that engaged employees are proven to be more productive. *Disengaged employees cost US businesses a staggering amount each year. A recent joint study that surveyed 1,500 respondents put the figure between $450 and $550 *billion*.

The benefits for internal stakeholders are clear—a strong, healthy company culture drives productivity and raises profitability. This motivation has been clear for decades, but recently business executives' motivation to consider the impact of their company culture expanded to include the interests of *external* stakeholders, as well. Investors and consumers (and even the government) are now interested in whether or not the organizations they do business with:

1. Have values that are aligned with theirs, and
2. Can validate frontline leaders and employees demonstrate acceptable behaviors that align with those values.

Every other day a story hits the newsfeed about a celebrity falling from grace. A highly offensive tweet, from fifteen or twenty years ago, was suddenly uncovered, and as soon as the public found out, the offending celebrity lost followers, was dropped by their sponsors, and in some cases lost their employment. Investors no longer wanted to fund them, and consumers no longer wanted to buy from them.

Investors and consumers in the current market are similar. They want to see the organizations they back, or buy from, embody values they agree with.

We have come to a crossroads that has been in construction for the past two decades. How organizations truly embody the values they claim has become paramount to their company culture and operational performance. This point brings us to the fundamental challenge facing business leaders today.

Many organizations publicly tout their company values—like diversity, inclusion, fairness, integrity, and even trust—only to reveal, through their own practices, that these values represent nothing more than a window dressing to appeal to the marketplace. Their values have become lofty words without any meaningful practice.

With changes to the labor market and enhanced interest in social movements, organizations worldwide are now required (or feel forced) to address the statements their business executives make surrounding the values they espouse, versus the actions they actually display. They have to get real about their culture.

If this is you:

- **Will this realization make some of you uncomfortable?** Definitely.

- **Is recognizing this reality and pushing through that discomfort necessary?** Absolutely.
- **Is taking real and meaningful action to address the reality that you can't fake your company culture any longer an optional choice?** No!

It's time to get real, raw, and candid about your company culture. Getting real means diving into honest and fearless self-reflection. It means turning an unblinking eye on how we lead and contribute to defining, implementing, measuring, and improving our company culture.

Ask yourself:

> Do I, as an executive in my organization, know how to facilitate the process for realizing my desired company "culture"?

If your answer is "No," "I don't know," or "I'm not sure," then you should keep reading. This book will introduce you to a new system (culture performance management) and a way to implement and maintain it. CultureWorx is a software platform geared to help you select your values, and define and sustain acceptable behaviors to go along with them.

Most companies don't know how to foster the company culture they advocate. Company values should dictate employee and leadership behaviors, which should inform how they engage, interact, and make decisions. This is the foundation on which company culture is built.

The definition and display of company culture is often misrepresented as nonpractical or is disconnected from what is considered a critical component to achieving one's core business objectives.

For example, we recently engaged with one of America's best-loved breweries who shared with us the progress they have made with their leadership to increase employee engagement survey scores. This brewery has been able to elevate their engagement survey scores into the ninetieth percentile range. They decided to use these scores as one of the primary criteria for internal ranking of plant performance company-wide. On the surface, this approach seems practical and very connected to their business, right? Let's look a little closer at this example, as we reflected further on the conversation with one of the top executives at this business ("The Brewery").

Here's how the conversation evolved:

The Brewery: "We've really made a lot of progress on our culture. We take a lot of pride in our employee engagement survey and we've focused a lot of time and energy to increase that score."

They pointed to a list of plants on the presentation on their laptop and focused on the one at the top.

"This plant used to have an employee experience score in the sixties. Today, the score is in the nineties."

Us: "It sounds like your company culture and plant performance are right where you want them, then."

The Brewery: "Well…not exactly."

Us: "What do you mean?"

The Brewery: "Frankly, our performance isn't good, and our frontline leaders don't know how to communicate and engage with their team members."

Us: "Help us understand how your employee experience score is in the nineties, but your performance is lacking and your people don't possess the skills to engage with their employees. How is that possible?"

They then gave us a couple of potential reasons:

1. Frontline leaders don't know how to effectively communicate and engage with frontline employees.
2. Frontline employees don't have respect for leadership because leadership doesn't know how to engage them.

Us: "It sounds like you aren't connecting your leaders' behaviors and performance to how you measure your company culture. It could be that your values aren't clearly defined."

We pointed out that there seemed to be a disconnect between what they wanted and how they were measuring it. What they *were* measuring didn't align with the culture they desired—management believed they were acting in accordance with the company's values, but their definitions weren't aligned. When we told them that, a light bulb went off, as if we were introducing them to running water.

The Brewery: "We've never really thought of it that way."

Like many of our past clients, the Brewery's intentions were good, but their leadership engagement measurement wasn't connected to how they expected their leaders to behave. Their engagement score was high, but their leaders weren't behaving consistently and acceptably. This is why performance was low. They weren't measuring company culture effectively, because they were focused on employees' individualized, circumstantial, and often misaligned perceptions of how leaders engaged with them and not actual *leadership* engagement, which has been validated in real time and measured against a standard for culture performance management.

WHY CULTURE PERFORMANCE MANAGEMENT?

To effectively measure company culture, we need to measure the *leaders'* behaviors and how well *they* are engaging with employees, not the other way around. In other words, the wrong definition results in the wrong actions and misappropriated investments when attempting to drive change.

Many organizations aren't correctly defining company culture, so they can't effectively measure it. For them, company culture is observed through a technical lens, and it's considered nonessential to business execution.

On the other hand, business executives across all industry verticals who realize the importance—better yet, the necessity—of examining their company culture appreciate its effect on their business. But they often fall short when defining the origin, meaning, and impact of their company culture on their organization and the community. For many of these executives, company culture means deploying tools like employee experience surveys, hosting company events, and promoting team building. For others, they believe they need to do more beyond the traditional "culture initiatives," but don't know how. Where on the spectrum of action do you fall?

Most business leaders have come to the realization that people need to feel a sense of belonging. We can attribute this to the bottom three layers of Maslow's Hierarchy of Needs:

Self-Actualization
Desire to become the
most that one can be

Esteem
Respect, self-esteem, status,
recognition, strength, freedom

Love and Belonging
Friendship, intimacy, family,
sense of connection

Safety Needs
Personal security,
employment, resources,
health, property

Physiological Needs
Air, water, food, shelter,
sleep, clothing,
reproduction

Team building, company events, and surveys are initiatives that are important to internal stakeholders because they foster the fulfillment of the physiological and safety-centric needs of individuals. However, to drive real and true culture performance management, executives must take it a step further. It is critical that leaders apply an organized and systematic approach to defining, implementing, measuring, and improving their company culture. This is only possible through the adoption of CultureWorx, our proposed culture performance management platform. As far as we know, there isn't another system that aligns values and behaviors and can be practiced, evaluated, and measured in real time.

Culture Performance Management (CPM): *Culture performance management refers to the system for aligning an organization's core company values with specific and actionable leadership behaviors that can be practiced, evaluated, and measured in real time in order to drive immediate improvement in how leaders engage, interact, and make decisions. The ultimate objective is to foster short-interval and continuous improvement of one's company culture. This is achieved through the implementation of a comprehensive CPM that connects leadership engagement and work execution touchpoints that ultimately influence business performance outcomes. CPM is designed to support the sustainability of performance results. It also provides visibility into the progress leaders make toward practicing the behaviors that serve as an ideal company culture requisite.*

Culture performance management is not only essential—it's at the core of an organization's ability to succeed and turn a sizable profit because it creates consistency and predictability in one's business. Frontline leaders (anyone in a leadership role who isn't functioning in a purely strategic capacity) are the main drivers of company culture. However, is it reasonable for you, as a senior leader, to expect your frontline leaders to exhibit consistent, acceptable, and optimal behaviors that are reflective of your organization's values if those behaviors and values haven't been defined and taught? No.

Very few companies knowingly employ unprincipled people or set out on an unethical mission.

Culture performance management enables executives to define and measure their company culture so they can address issues before they arise. It creates consistency and stability and allows for scalability.

Growing and scaling require predictability and replication. Executive leadership focused on those goals must establish behavioral standards across the company. Without a standard, predictability is uncertain and repetition is nearly impossible.

However, simply hanging your values on the kitchen wall isn't enough. You've set a standard, but how do you measure it? Also, what are the *standards* of that measurement?

A culture performance management system fulfills your desire to create one standard for your optimal company culture.

MANAGE YOUR CULTURE DIFFERENTLY

One company culture. That's the dream, isn't it? Or, maybe the dream is a better culture. Whatever the motivation, there is an old but true saying:

If you *want* something different, you have to *do* something different.

Most company cultures are decidedly mediocre. Yours doesn't have to be, but an evolution in assessing company culture is needed. Frontline leaders and employees need better direction and recognition, because the companies with the lowest team member attrition and the least amount of open positions (because they fill so quickly) are typically the companies with the strongest company cultures. This means the organization's culture vision is fulfilled by the leaders who understand and *practice* the behaviors that embody their company values, ultimately influencing their business results.

Value embodiment is perpetuated most impactfully at the front line. This book was written to proactively address how frontline leaders engage with frontline employees.

We want to share the story of how our culture performance management system was invented.

The year was 2012. Our team was selected to engage with one of the top ten largest private companies in the United States. We were brought in by a senior-level leader who genuinely wanted to invest in the skill and effectiveness of the frontline leadership team. This leader saw that these frontline leaders were challenged and struggling daily to achieve the quantity (and quality) of production this facility was designed to achieve.

There was chaos, and firefighting, every day. It was the same problems over and over again, which resulted in:

- Lost capacity utilization
- Higher material and labor costs than planned
- Lower yields than expected
- Out-of-balance inventories
- Missed customer commitments
- High transportation costs

Not even the equipment was properly set up, nor cared for, to achieve the reliability needed to keep it running. Plant leadership was frustrated, almost as much as the employees.

Respect, trust, and engagement were low. Communication was poor, or absent, because teams worked in silos. Shift leaders called out other shift leaders, or remained silent.

It didn't stop there. There was poor understanding of managing the processes, so department leaders were frustrated with each other. There was even *poorer* understanding and utilization of the systems the company had developed to help manage processes, production, and performance. The data in the systems was unreliable, so it was rarely used for decision-making and problem-solving. Employee turnover was high and contributed to instability and low performance. The culture was chaotic, yet the local management team eagerly wanted to improve.

Through all the chaos, frustration, and poor performance, this senior leader had a single motivation and objective:

I want to bring dignity and respect to the frontline leaders.

The senior leader asked calmly, so one question was asked in return:

"Why do you want to bring dignity and respect to the frontline leaders?"

"My father was a truck driver, you know, a blue-collar kind of guy. He worked hard every day and sacrificed to provide us what we needed. No glory. Just hard work.

"I had the highest level of dignity and respect for my father, and I want to build up my frontline leaders so their team members have the same level of dignity and respect for them. Right now, our employees have very little, if any, respect or trust for our frontline leaders, and this is my responsibility to fix. It is my duty to develop these leaders and implement a culture of respect and dignity."

There was no mention from the senior leader of productivity or cost improvement. They absolutely wanted to improve performance, but that was not the primary motivation—it was to fix the culture. Our partner knew performance improvement would follow.

We got the engagement, but we knew we only had one shot with this company, so we made sure to hit a home run. That first engagement went so well, we earned the right to partner with *all eight* of this leader's sites, and subsequently, we were asked to move into other divisions. We've established twenty-six partnerships with this company over the span of six years.

We spent an abundant amount of time partnering with this company—the partnership started in 2012 and ran through 2017. We were privy to this company's insider workings from the top floor to the shop floor. We had relationships with frontline employees and members of the C-level inner circle. So, we were able to gain knowledge and insights into what decisions were made and why. We had intimate knowledge of company data, differing opinions, and motivations for employees of all levels, across the entire organization.

The idea for our culture performance management system was created during our work with this partner. Many ideas are created from an original idea that didn't quite solve the intended problem—advancement birthed from adversity, so to speak. CPM is one of those ideas.

Based on academic research in social learning theory (Dr. Vaughn's specialty), empirical evidence, and twenty-five years of real-life, practical experience in operational performance, *From Culture to Culture* provides a candid look at the pillars of the culture performance management system we developed for accurately defining, implementing, measuring, and improving company culture.

The book aims to disrupt the market's perception of what corporate culture *really* means and show readers how to leverage it as a tool to operationalize business. It is a culmination of the best practices and corporate culture research we've been cultivating for years.

From Culture to Culture is ideologically neutral. Its purpose is not to help you figure out whether or not your current culture is "good" or "bad." It has nothing to do with that. This book is about helping your organization take the steps necessary to connect your company values to proven leadership behaviors and connection points (that optimize business outcomes), and determining whether or not they align with your company's values.

OPERATIONALIZE YOUR COMPANY CULTURE

From an academic perspective, the study of culture is broad, and from an organizational leadership context, it's a huge unknown. Culture has always been centered on the employee experience, leadership-employee engagement, and human capital management strategy, but has never been viewed through an operational lens. Company culture has yet to be widely operationalized.

This book presents a system, driven by behavior, for operationalizing company culture. It will teach you why it's paramount to own your company culture—its development, the results it yields (or in most cases, doesn't), and its influence on the roles and responsibilities of every employee within the organization. It will also stress the importance of the daily active management and improvement of company culture, funneled from executive leadership down to the front lines.

From Culture to Culture is a journey of acknowledgement and recognition. The way most companies manage company culture is ineffective and has led to organizational challenges—this book provides organizations with the mechanisms to examine their company culture and introduces them to a validated system to define, implement, and measure it.

It isn't a step-by-step or how-to book because it would take an additional five hundred pages of explanation. Our system is backed by nuanced, empirical research and observational data and is very detailed. This book is the articulation of our cultural performance management system, not the details about how it works.

Our CPM system applies the principles of proactive leadership to connect an organization's core company values to the behavioral indicators that influence employee experiences. It's a methodology *and* technology that gathers and captures actual, real-time, behavioral data where culture happens—on the front line between leaders and their employees (not lagging indicators of how employees *think* their leaders behave).

The lack of cultural operationalization is a massive gap in the marketplace that this book aspires to bridge. It articulates the practical application of behaviors that drive cultural norms in an organization, but does so in a manner that can influence outcomes proactively. There are certain behaviors that optimize business, and those behaviors are very similar to the behaviors that optimize culture. The CPM system outlined in this book drives cultural change because it connects leadership, behaviors, practices, and interactions to business performance outcomes.

From Culture to Culture is also a guide for achieving your ideal company culture and turning it into a company "X factor" for talent acquisition and retention. Money is no longer a primary motivator for candidates seeking employment or current employees seeking growth—they want company engagement, a mission statement they agree with, and core values they can get behind. Current external market conditions are forcing companies to address the sustainability of their business practices, talent acquisition, and talent retention, emphasizing how leaders engage employees.

Company culture is the substance of how your frontline leadership and team members engage and interact with one another. It is the culmination of all the existing customs, interactions, connections, and dynamics in your business, as well as the attitudes, behaviors, and characteristics of your frontline leaders and employees.

In many of today's businesses, there is a major disconnect between how engagement is measured and actively managed. However, the lack of management systems for company culture can be attributed to the disconnect many leaders discover between how leaders actually influence employee performance and, ultimately, the business results. This book articulates the path to achieve cultural consciousness and integrity, optimal performance results, and increased talent acquisition and retention through effective culture performance management.

Most company executives, across every industry vertical, are talking about corporate culture and why it's essential. These executives are quickly realizing they can no longer fake their company culture, but few have succeeded in operationalizing their vision.

Let's explore why this happens in Part 1, "You Can't Fake Company Culture."

PART 1

YOU CAN'T FAKE COMPANY CULTURE

CHAPTER 1

SHOW ME THE CULTURE!

Jerry Maguire is a 1996 film starring Tom Cruise, Cuba Gooding Jr., and Renee Zellweger. It was directed by Cameron Crowe and grossed $274 million worldwide. Considering the film's budget was $50 million, it was considered a financial success.

It was a critical success, too. *Jerry Maguire* was nominated for five Academy Awards, three Screen Actors Guild (SAG) Awards, and two Golden Globes; Cruise won a Golden Globe for the title role and Gooding won both a SAG award *and* an Academy Award for "Best/Outstanding Male in a Supporting Role."

For both fans and critics, *Jerry Maguire* was the standout movie of the year, and Gooding the standout star. All of his scenes with Cruise were fantastic, but the scene toward the beginning of the film, when they're negotiating a partnership, is legendary. Gooding finally agrees to partner with a desperate Cruise because Cruise says, repeatedly:

Show me the money!

Show me the money!

SHOW me the MONEY!

SHOW ME THE MONEY!

Cruise says it louder and louder until he screams the words into the receiver. (This was 1996, remember? Landline phones were still in full use.) With that, Gooding is satisfied and asks Cruise to be his agent.

Gooding wants to be convinced Cruise's interest in him isn't a facade. Gooding wants to know whether Cruise's interest in him as an athlete is real and genuine, and that he'll work hard to make Gooding as much money as possible.

That scene is one of the most memorable scenes in the film—it establishes an authentic relationship between the two lead characters.

BEHAVIOR ALWAYS REVEALS THE TRUTH

The relationship between Cruise and Gooding in *Jerry Maguire* wasn't fake. It was real and genuine and is what made their partnership a success.

In today's business world, instead of "Show me the money!" existing employees, frontline leaders, and potential new recruits are saying, "Show me the culture!" Partners, suppliers, vendors, and *consumers* are reciting it, too.

But for many businesses, company culture has become a facade. They know it's important, and even business-critical in some instances, but creating one that's real, effective, and measurable is daunting at best and impossible at worst. So, instead of working toward cultivating a company culture that's sincere and honest, they create values and definitions they *think* will satisfy both internal and external stakeholders but don't connect to the company's mission and purpose.

Which is a lot like putting new lipstick on the same pig!

A decade ago, these companies may have been able to get away with faking company culture, but any attempts today are going to fall short. Whether it's an entry-level employee calling BS on a supervisor, or a frontline leader calling out senior management, if the company culture is fake, the stakeholders are going to know. Partners and customers want to partner with a company they believe in, and if they believe a company's culture is fake, they'll call it out.

Behavior always reveals the truth. You know the old saying: "If it walks like a duck and talks like a duck (quack, quack!), it's a duck." When the behaviors of employees and leaders don't align with the desired company culture, it sticks out like a sore thumb—everyone who interacts with the organization can instantly tell.

That's why you can't fake company culture. If you try, everyone you interact with will call you out.

THE FIVE MYTHS OF COMPANY CULTURE... DEBUNKED!

A genuine, authentic company culture is needed in today's workplace to attract and retain talent, drive employee engagement, and increase profitability. Most organizations find themselves in a cycle of creating or perpetuating a "fake" culture, because they fall victim to believing company culture myths.

Cultivating a real company culture is difficult enough *without* false information circling overhead, yet there are five myths that make this task even more challenging.

Here are some of the fundamental misconceptions we hear a lot. It's time to put these myths to rest.

MYTH 1: COMPANY CULTURE SHOULD DEVELOP "ORGANICALLY."

Organizational culture takes root through the values, associated behaviors, and interactions between individuals within an organization. If the core values and principles by which an organization's team members should operate are not predefined (and "managed"), leaders and subordinates will behave in a manner that they (subjectively) believe to be right.

These personal beliefs are usually the product of learned behaviors and experiences that may be misaligned or (more often) inconsistent with driving a sustainable and results-oriented culture that is right for the business.

We like to frame this as the difference between "managed culture" and "organic culture."

Company culture left to happen organically won't consistently reflect company values because the definitions of those values will all be different. Organic cultures have many employees who believe they behave acceptably, but without a set of explicitly defined behaviors, those behaviors *will* vary.

Likewise, don't confuse a "managed culture" with a "mechanistic culture," in which hierarchy and bureaucracy become the pillars to communication and practice.

Truth: *A "managed culture" means that senior leaders of an organization make a deliberate and purposeful effort to define and embody the values that drive the organization's mission and vision of how it serves its internal and external stakeholders to achieve defined business outcomes.*

MYTH 2: EMPLOYEE FEEDBACK IS THE BEST MEASURE OF COMPANY CULTURE.

This one may surprise you, but while employee feedback does provide some insight into employee experience, it's not the ultimate measure of company culture.

The most significant weakness of employee feedback is that each employee provides their feedback based on their own personal definition and experience. When an employee responds to a key cultural value such as *trust*, they respond based on their own definition and personal experience with trust. Their personal standard is then used as a measurement.

When a company uses surveys, they receive responses based on as many standards as there are employees. Using rolled-up data to change leadership behaviors is a real problem because every employee's standard is different.

Worse than this, each individual's standard is unknown. Even if leadership understood each employee's unique value definition, and asked employees to go interact with each other in a way that matches (and satisfies) their individual definition, they would end up with a lot of different individual cultures.

This reality would be the opposite of what most companies desire:

> One culture where all leadership and employees communicate and interact using the same set of company values.

The problem with lagging, rather than immediate feedback, is that it is often circumstantial, one-directional, and predicated on an individual's personal perceptions, feelings, or emotions. Feedback collection cuts out the full scope of interactions, the crucial back-and-forth that exists at all levels of an organization.

Employee feedback captures a narrow vantage point and perspective. It fails to explore the true implications of positive or negative personal interactions that convey the full impact of an organization's culture on a business.

Truth: *A healthy workplace culture will be sculpted by the values, behaviors, and interactions between stakeholders, from senior leaders to the front line and back again. Fix the culture, and the employee experience will fix itself.*

MYTH 3: THE HIGHER THE PAY, THE BETTER THE CULTURE.

Robert Half published findings from an extensive survey of twelve thousand workers that found that "culture, respect, and pride" were three of the most significant factors in job satisfaction.[1]

Companies that use compensation as an indicator of culture also rely on "employee satisfaction" as their measure of cultural performance, which, as noted in Myth 2, is not a best practice.

---

1   Kristen Bahler, "Want to Be Happier at Work? Look for a Job with These Traits," Money.com, October 28, 2016, https://money.com/employees-happy-new-research/.

The whole notion that pay equals better culture is antiquated and misaligned with today's workforce. As confirmed through numerous studies, employees (especially millennials) desire engagement, positive personal experiences, interactions, a feeling of connection, belonging, etc. These factors, not compensation, correlate most directly to company culture.

The actual rate of pay should not be the indicator of an organization's cultural performance. An employee may be happy with their pay and stick around, but the company culture contributes to a negative work or life experience.

Truth: *Culture should be defined first. Pay is simply a nuance that will influence an employee's experience but does not directly impact company culture without other factors involved, such as equity, fairness, integrity, inclusivity, etc.*

MYTH 4: COMPANY CULTURE DOES NOT EQUAL COMPANY PERFORMANCE.

We could probably cite four novellas worth of statistics to directly contradict the above falsehood. Study after study has shown that company culture correlates directly to performance outcomes, making it crucial to invest in a true management strategy. According to Callan, companies ranked highly on company culture report a four times higher success rate, 21 percent greater profitability, 24 percent less turnover, and 14 percent greater productivity than those ranked lower on the culture scale.

Soak that in for a minute. How has your culture impacted your operational performance?

Consider the additional fact that 90 percent of employees at companies with great culture express confidence in their leadership—it's a win for executives to adopt a strategy to actively measure, manage, and scale their culture.

The values, behaviors, and interactions between individuals within an organization set the tone for how everyone approaches their day—the decisions they make, the efforts they apply to their work, how they strive to overcome performance barriers—the list goes on and on.

These factors influence how quickly, efficiently, and effectively an organization can maintain optimal performance and fulfill its mission. Less efficiency, reduced optimization, and limited capacity all diminish a company's bottom line.

Truth: *Culture is not the "soft side" of an organization. Rather, it is the concrete foundation which supports or drives an organization's performance. It dictates the foundation, the framework, the windows, and the upkeep of the whole house!*

MYTH 5: THERE IS A "RIGHT" OR A "WRONG" COMPANY CULTURE.

We work with a wide variety of companies in a wide range of industries, from food and beverage manufacturing to pharmaceutical to automotive. As a result, we know for a fact that culture is not "one size fits all." For example, some companies have a very team-oriented culture with participation from workers at all levels, whereas others have a more formal or traditional work culture. Other companies, like Google (a small startup you may have heard of), have an informal or nontraditional culture.

Whatever the construct of your company culture, the overall performance of your company is, and will continue to be, impacted by it. Nonetheless, you don't have to force yourself to be the next Google or Amazon to land on what works for you.

Truth: *Every business is different, and so every business's definition of its culture will be unique.*

ALIGNMENT AND TRUST GO HAND IN HAND

Myths create distrust and work to perpetuate suspicion. When people believe one thing, but see or experience another, they get confused and don't know what is true or what to trust.

This is especially true of company culture. If your values and definitions state one thing but employee behavior, at all levels, demonstrates another, that misalignment will be noticeable. It will also make it difficult for you to be trusted. Today's workforce wants an employer with a mission and values they believe in and demonstrated values they can *see*.

"Show me the culture!" is more than a play on a popular movie phrase from the mid-1990s—it's also a reference to demonstrable behaviors.

Show me the culture.

Show me the acceptable behaviors that align with the definitions of the company's values.

Alignment and trust go hand in hand, and a lack of trust can lead to problems with your company culture.

The establishment and sustainability of trusting relationships is the foundation of how they effectively communicate and inter-act with one another; trust serves as the catalyst for achieving a healthy company culture.

Any factor that contributes to a breakdown in communication becomes paramount to constructive human interactions. Ulti-mately, constructive human interactions are predicated on a shared assumption. Many assume leaders of an organization will act honestly and truthfully, with reliability and predictability, which is at the heart of any business leader's objective. Business performance reliability and predictability is all rooted in trust!

We're living in a post-truth era where trust is difficult to earn yet impossible to move forward without. More on broken trust in the next chapter.

CASE STUDY: CULTURE IS REAL

We have clients who are major product wholesalers and dis-tributors—they either produce white labels for brand products or sell them directly. One of these clients worked with a global wholesaler that showed up randomly for a culture audit to determine whether to continue the partnership. The auditors compared the live feedback they heard on the floor to our client's mission and values to see if they aligned; they wanted to see if our clients could walk the walk.

Our client was used to audits focused on food safety and pro-duction standards, but this type of audit was new. We weren't working with them on cultural performance management at the time, so we could only lay witness to their reaction to the impending audit. They tried to map out the auditor's journey throughout the facility—where they would go and who they would talk to—but it was no use. The auditor intentionally asked to speak to the employees on the floor *without* execu-tive management and frontline leadership staring over their shoulder, and once they did, it was all over. Those employees revealed the truth about the organization—that frontline lead-ers didn't engage employees.

When you ask your frontline leaders and employees the right questions, their opinions about the company are valid.

- "Does your manager interact and engage with you?"
- "What is your impression of your manager?"
- "Do you witness your manager behaving in accordance with the company values?"

However, remember that surveys are still lagging indicators of culture, and they certainly cannot predict behavior. They are reactive. Proactive company culture management requires examining values and behaviors at the source. It means behavioral alignment between executive management and frontline leaders and employees.

CHAPTER 2

BROKEN TRUST

When you think of the pop music duo Milli Vanilli, what's the first thing that comes to your mind?

(If you're thinking "lip-sync scandal"—Ding! Ding! Ding! Move to the head of the class.)

In 1989, Milli Vanilli was on a fast track to success. Their song "Girl You Know It's True" was on the Billboard Hot 100 for twenty-six weeks, and they were asked to tour with R & B singer Paula Abdul and rapper Tone Loc. The music community considered Fab Morvan and Rob Pilatus (Milli Vanilli) legitimate artists.

That legitimacy was turned on its head when the tour landed at Lake Compounce amusement park in Bristol, Connecticut. During their act, the chorus of their hit song started to skip… revealing that the two "singers" were actually lip-syncing.

Word didn't travel as quickly back then as it does today, so Milli Vanilli went on to win three American Music Awards and the Grammy for Best New Artist in 1990. When the music video for "Girl You Know It's True" came out, it was a big success and made the band widely recognizable. They also had four more hit songs: "Blame It on the Rain," "Girl I'm Gonna Miss You," "Baby Don't Forget My Number," and "All or Nothing."

Their stardom didn't last much longer though, because people grew suspicious of the duo; during interviews, reporters found it odd that they had French and German accents and didn't believe they sang their own songs; the voices in the interviews didn't match the voices on the recordings. The rumors got so bad that their label, Arista Records, paid for a dialect coach to help narrow the accent gap, so the voices sounded more similar. In the end it didn't matter, though, and Milli Vanilli put a stop to interviews altogether.

When Milli Vanilli was dropped by Arista Records in late 1990, it was revealed they not only lip-synced their songs in concert, they didn't sing on the songs' recordings, either. The vocals were sung by Brad Howell and John Davis, *not* Fab Morvan and Rob Pilatus. The Grammys didn't take the misrepresentation too well, so they revoked their 1990 Best New Artist award.

Milli Vanilli broke the trust of the music industry *and* the general public. They went from a pop music sensation to a complete laughing stock overnight and never made a comeback.[2]

DO YOUR FRONTLINE LEADERS LIP-SYNC YOUR CULTURE?

Once trust is broken, it's a long road back. Sometimes, the road is permanently closed. Just ask Milli Vanilli. They misrepresented themselves and faked their singing skills, and once everyone found out, they fell (hard) from pop music grace.

---

2   Rachel Chang, "Milli Vanilli's Lip-Sync Scandal: Inside One of Music's Biggest Hoaxes," Biography.com, July 8, 2020, https://www.biography.com/news/milli-vanilli-lip-sync-scandal.

That was thirty years ago. Today, people are especially distrustful and everything can be captured on video. If someone says one thing yet does another, there's a real possibility they will be called out for being "fake."

The same goes for company culture. Hearing one thing but seeing another is confusing and creates misalignment. How can frontline employees be expected to demonstrate acceptable behaviors, as defined by the company's values, when they *see* frontline leaders acting differently. This misalignment leads to value misrepresentation and cultural corruption.

> **Cultural Corruption:** *An unaligned workforce resulting in negative impacts on morale, productivity, efficiency, and overall organizational interactions that are based upon behaviors, exhibited by company leaders, and are misrepresentative of the ideal company culture.*

We're not talking about political or financial corruption—we're talking about erosion, like a car muffler that rusts out over time. Cultural corruption happens slowly and it's never planned.

Employees expect to see certain behaviors from their leaders. When they witness behavior that is the opposite of what they anticipated, they infer the company is dishonest or fraudulent. This may not be conscious, but when employees work in a misaligned environment, establishing trust is difficult.

How many of your frontline leaders are lip-syncing your company culture? When you ask them a question about your company culture, do they repeat the same words over and over?

CORRUPTION ISN'T INTENTIONAL

When employees feel fooled and deceived by frontline leaders, engagement suffers and poor performance increases. Most leaders aren't doing this intentionally—they believe they're behaving in accordance with the company's values. This results when values aren't uniformly selected, and the accompanying behaviors aren't defined and taught; both the employee and the leader think the other is corrupt in their intentions. Effective and clear communication, which results in shared understanding, requires standard definitions. This is the only way the meaning of the message is received with shared understanding. When the definitions between the sender and receiver are the same, there is clear communication, which builds trust between the sender and the receiver. When they aren't clear, there is miscommunication and mistrust. Clear communication and trust lead to a shared understanding.

Language and communication are the foundation of every company culture. The shared understanding of words used in a company culture is foundational for it to properly function. Individuals who are a part of the shared understanding can function appropriately and survive. Those who aren't will have a difficult time, unless they learn the language.

What do people first recognize when they travel to a foreign country and step off their plane or train, or get out of their car? Most likely, it's the citizens of that country speaking a different language.

If you spoke the language, you know the trip would be more enjoyable because it would be easier to communicate with the locals. Asking for directions, menu recommendations, or travel help would be simple because you share a language.

On the other hand, when you don't speak the language, almost everything is more difficult. You might find yourself in an embarrassing situation, like entering the wrong restroom.

Cultural corruption is fueled by ineffective communication and misunderstanding, which only increases frustrations and mistrust. The likely outcome is behavioral misalignment, and failed expectations.

Cultural corruption can also be a slow burn. Many things change over time, and these changes are often out of our control. Sometimes the original reasons for the creation and definition of a company value is lost, and those values, terms, and definitions become outdated.

Take the value *commitment*, for example, defined as:

> Commitment means showing up to the office every day, on time, ready to perform at your best.

Prior to the global COVID-19 pandemic, this value definition may have made sense. However, in response to the government's attempt to control the outbreak and promote the safety of others, many companies had to create remote-working policies for their employees to keep their businesses going. Considering the aforementioned definition of *commitment* as a core value, if an organization fails to update its definition and application to the business, internal and external stakeholders may deem their culture corrupt. When an organization continues to practice those values without reexamining or redefining them, it presents as another con to employees.

Let's look at another example for clarity. This is a definition of *dedication* from a list of company values created by a client in 2000:

Dedication means doing everything necessary to get the job done to the customer's full satisfaction. It means putting in the work, day after day, and constantly striving for perfection.

This definition may not resonate with a modern-day workforce, especially if the organization's mission, purpose, and values have been updated to reflect current workforce sentiments. Let's try this definition on for size, instead:

Dedication means enthusiasm for our company's mission, purpose, and values.

Those are very different definitions that elicit very different behaviors.

Cultural corruption usually isn't intentional—most of the time it just happens. Remember when the original Atari gaming console was released in 1977? Or Nintendo in 1983? Everyone thought those systems were going to last forever, but the tech advanced and they were replaced by better machines and gaming software. Company values are a lot like those gaming systems—in time, they can become erroneous and obsolete. To keep playing the company culture game, they need a serious upgrade.

This doesn't mean the premise or intent behind the core values that make up your company culture must change. Like gaming systems, enhancing the application and functionality of components that make up your company culture ultimately enhances the employee (user) experience. However, the mission and core objectives remain the same. Also unintentionally, behavior considered to be "acceptable" can erode and corrupt over time, too. Sometimes through our own *subconscious* actions and behaviors, we debase values unknowingly. Albeit unintentional, the result is still the same—values and behaviors that are misaligned.

We aren't trying to transfer accountability around corruption, but we *are* saying that subconscious actions sometimes also cause corruption, especially generationally. What was acceptable in 1960, for example, may not be acceptable today. The world is changing so quickly that if you defined your culture's acceptable behaviors more than five to ten years ago, we strongly recommend you reevaluate them; they may not still hold true.

Values and behaviors should evolve over time because they should be applicable *today*.

CULTURE IS HAPPENING, WITH OR WITHOUT YOU

Company culture is happening, whether the values are set and defined or not. When executive members of management expect to see certain behaviors and don't, it's difficult for them to understand—it's a culture conundrum.

> **Culture Conundrum:** *Having an organizational company culture contrary to what is desired by executive leadership—wishing for one type of company culture but having somehow ended up with another.*

When a culture conundrum exists, in most cases both the leaders *and* frontline employees are innocent. Neither are wrong—they both believe they're acting according to their own definition. This happens when no one can pinpoint the origin of the existing culture.

So, where does the problem reside?

If you believe the myths about culture covered in Chapter 1 and abide by them, that's a problem you need to solve. Perhaps your employees aren't engaged and you have high churn, your profits don't hit the margins your stakeholders demand, or your reputation in the market is less than stellar. While you may believe these situations drive the company culture, the root cause is typically one (or more!) of the following three mistakes—you'll notice they correlate to the myths.

1. THE PROBLEM HASN'T BEEN FRAMED CORRECTLY.

In the case of corporate culture, problem-solvers start with the employee experience first and work their way backward toward leadership behavior.

That isn't the way the water flows, though—it should be flipped. Our leaders' behaviors should match our company values, so our employee experience is correct. The analysis should first start with leadership behavior and whether or not it aligns with the company's core values.

2. INFORMATION IS MISSING.

Sometimes information is missing. If a jigsaw puzzle has 500 pieces but you can only find 499, can you solve it?

No, because you're missing the final piece.

In the case of culture performance management, there are often two pieces missing: the definition of the values *and* their accompanying behaviors. A conundrum exists because neither managers nor frontline leaders know how to act.

3. THERE IS NO CULTURE PERFORMANCE MANAGEMENT SYSTEM IN PLACE.

It's also hard to solve the culture conundrum without a methodology or a culture performance management system. Why has the employee engagement needle remained stagnant for the last ten years? Because no one measures, monitors, and refines employee engagement in real time.

We see culture conundrums all the time—and executive leadership doesn't know how to fix them. Why is their company culture contrary to the culture they want? Because they haven't defined their company values and acceptable behaviors or taught their frontline leaders how to practice them.

This is usually seen in two different ways:

1. Employees demonstrate behaviors opposite of what executive leadership define as acceptable.
2. Managers demonstrate behaviors as defined by their own experiences, which may not align with the employees' personal definitions.

Each instance creates a negative experience for employees and managers. However, neither the manager nor the employee is wrong—they don't know the behaviors that executive leadership connects with the organization's core values. This has caused a culture conundrum, evidenced by the fact that the mean employee engagement score hasn't moved more than a few points (in either direction) for the past decade.

Effective, long-lasting improvements to culture can't be made with lagging data or *without* a tool to fine-tune acceptable behaviors in real time.

When it comes to managing workplace culture, people are confused by what perpetuates it and why it exists. Unfounded cultures and subcultures emerge within an organization when value and behavior origins are unknown and aren't linked to day-to-day, direct and indirect interactions between team members.

A managed culture ensures that appropriate values and associated behaviors—as defined by the leaders—manifest throughout an organization, and that the right leadership practices are in place to reinforce these values through practical actions and decision-making tactics.

Culture has been happening, with or without organizational leadership in tow, for a long time. In our more than twenty-five years of either partnering with companies to help them improve their operational performance, or working in executive leadership roles for major organizations, we have yet to see a company that has solved the culture conundrum, because in our experience, value and behavior misalignment is rampant.

"WHAT DID YOU THINK OF YOUR SUPERVISOR?"

You may believe your company is one of the few organizations that *doesn't* have a culture conundrum to solve. We challenge you to review recent exit interviews.

When an employee leaves a company, a typical exit interview question is: "What did you think of your supervisor?"

Here are some of the most common responses:

- "They only talked to some people. They never came by to talk to me."

- "My supervisor isn't trustworthy."
- "My supervisor isn't fair and consistent."

If you see any of these responses in the exit interviews you review, your organization has a culture conundrum—your frontline leaders aren't behaving how you would expect.

Are they to blame, though? Were they given the tools needed to learn the company's values and the behaviors associated with each?

They don't have a culture performance management system to align with the values' definitions, so their company culture is constrained and can't reach its ideal state.

> **Cultural Constraint:** *The discrepancy between your ideal company culture and its current state, which results in negative behavioral impacts on morale, productivity, efficiency, and overall engagement. Most organizations are culturally constrained—they want to realize their ideal cultural state but don't have effective tools to do so.*

Cultural constraint happens when frontline leaders have been asked to do the best with what they've got. This leaves them directionless, though, like little pinballs bouncing around a pinball machine, hoping to score. In their heads, they believe they're behaving correctly, but the exit interviews reveal the opposite.

When you don't take the time to develop your frontline leaders around your culture, you've essentially abandoned them and left them to their own devices. Without standardized definitions, how can you expect them to behave uniformly and create the coveted one-company culture?

American engineer W. Edwards Deming, who helped create sampling techniques that the Bureau of Labor Statistics and the US Census Bureau still use today, astutely said:

> Eighty-five percent of the reasons for failure are deficiencies in systems and processes, rather than the people of leaders. The role of management is to change the process rather than badgering individuals to do better. The worker is not the problem. The system is the problem. If you want to improve performance, you must work on the system.[3]

The process is the problem, not the people. But without a culture performance management system in place, how can the process be measured and assessed?

THE SOLUTION IS CULTURE PERFORMANCE MANAGEMENT

People can adapt—they will rise to the occasion, as long as you develop them and give them a mechanism to understand and define company culture accurately, through behaviors that can't be faked. Culture performance management allows people to define and measure their culture, find the gaps within it, and act to fill them.

Milli Vanilli was one of the biggest pop bands in 1990, but they couldn't sing; they faked it and broke the trust of the general public *and* the music industry.

Trust is built on repeated experiences, which makes it difficult

---

3   M. Preston Leavitt, "Why 97.8 Percent of Your Organizations' Problems Are Not Due to Your People," LinkedIn.com, May 23, 2018, https://www.linkedin.com/pulse/why-978-your-organizations-problems-due-people-m-preston-leavitt/.

to earn. If frontline employees consistently see behaviors from frontline leaders that *don't* reflect the values' definitions they have in their heads, they'll be confused. This values-to-behaviors misalignment is a culture conundrum, leads to cultural corruption, and causes cultural constraint. All are problematic when establishing, managing, and scaling company culture.

The solution is culture performance management, but before we dig into the details of our system, we need to first fully grasp the difficulties facing the current market. We all know company culture is important to business growth, but to give it the attention it fully deserves, we need context.

In Chapter 3, "Understanding the Problems," we will break down the issues driving the rejuvenated focus on company culture and what we can do to fix them.

CHAPTER 3

UNDERSTANDING THE PROBLEMS

A study from Gallup in 2018 explored the percentage of US workers considered "actively engaged" by their leaders at their job, meaning they were considered to be enthusiastic, involved in the work-execution process and decision-making, and committed to their employer. The outcomes of the study revealed 34 percent of participants were considered engaged. This figure is tied for the highest level since Gallup began reporting the national figure in 2000.

Reason to celebrate, right?

Looking deeper reveals a different story. The annual percentage of engaged US workers moved from a low of 26 percent in 2000 and 2005 to 34 percent in 2018. Today, it's 32 percent. A fully engaged workforce increases business performance, reduces absenteeism, helps attract and retain talent, and sustains competitive advantage. It drives profitability and directly impacts an organization's bottom line. However, despite its ability to drive productivity and increase the bottom line, leader engagement has remained stagnant for decades.

So, why is this happening?

There are a few different theories to consider; however, we believe the metric hasn't moved for more than twenty years because of the antiquated methods applied when measuring leadership engagement *and* the ineffective approaches most leaders make to improve the outcome. Many companies use employee experience surveys, which generate lagging indicators that perpetuate reactive management responses to the results. If reactionary responses to these results aren't bad enough, to further compound the problem, these employee experience survey results (metrics) have become the primary measure of company culture performance and the driver of when, why, and how leaders attempt to improve this aspect of their business.

Typically, the results (statements of perceived experience) from these surveys, which were deployed to a sample or entire employee population, are examined, synthesized, and generalized to develop a list of "actions" or "focus areas" to drive improvement in their employee experiences, with the notion that these experiences reflect the culture of the organization.

Still don't see the issue with this approach?

Imagine trying to solve an equation where the variables don't align or agree with the numerical format that the outcome requires. In mathematics, to solve an equation is to find its solutions, which are the values that fulfill the condition stated by the equation, consisting generally of two expressions related by an equals sign. If the conditions and expressions all vary, the equation is impossible to solve! Now apply this concept to how company culture is measured today. Imagine taking the individualized and conditional opinions and perceived experiences of every employee (survey respondent) and attempting to identify themes (variables), then take those themes and equate them to what your leaders must do (in the future) to change the outcome of the equation. It's impossible!

Don't be confused by this problem. Employee experience surveys can play a vital role as a "checks and balances" tool to validate how your internal stakeholders perceive their leaders' engagement, only if your intent is to determine whether or not your culture performance management strategy has been effective, like advancing your learning and development resources for your frontline leadership.

Real-time assessment, measurement, and improvement of your leaders' engagement and decision-making requires a different approach. Rather than asking about company culture posthumously, a better question would be, *Are leadership behaviors aligned with the company's mission and values and are they exhibited right now?*

PROBLEM #1: IS YOUR CULTURE PERFORMANCE MANAGEMENT REACTIVE OR PROACTIVE?

Relying on lagging indicators is a *reactive* approach to company culture management. We believe employee experience surveys should work in congruence with a culture performance management system—they shouldn't be the only engagement measurement tool.

Are you exploring the impact of your company's culture through a reactive or proactive lens?

REACTIVE

Quite a few organizational leaders don't know how to measure or manage their company culture proactively, so they have adopted reactive methods to understand how their leaders drive their company culture vision. They use short-interval tools or the periodic solicitation of perceptions to drive insights about how the general population of employees or leaders perceives their experience.

However, the general nature and construct of these instruments yields reactive 'lagging' indicators of performance. They solicit reactive insights that include personal and anecdotal perceptions regarding individualized workplace experiences and opinions of leaders. These insights are often compiled, synthesized, and used to form generalizations about the organizational culture. These generalizations are then used as the basis for developing strategies to "improve" the workplace culture.

There are many issues with this approach. One fundamental issue is that the generalizations developed from these reactive insights are derived from the interpreter's casual correlations between employee perceptions and the performance outcomes of their leaders and the business. *There are no direct links that clarify and validate the specific factors contributing to the employee's perceptions (or misperceptions) of their experience.*

Root-cause analysis of the factors that contributed to the insights, and the objective linkage to the cultural performance of the company, never occurs. So, the cultural improvement strategies are reactive and circumstantial, and fail to have a sustainable impact.

To proactively measure workplace culture, understand how it translates into leader or business performance, and determine how to improve it, these reactive tools simply miss the mark.

PROACTIVE

A proactive response means it's time to step up and act. It means not waiting for lagging insights to serve as the sole indicators of how leaders are positively (or negatively) contributing to the employee experience.

It's a real-time approach to measuring how your leaders engage with employees and how those interactions align with your company culture.

Improving employee engagement begins with a proactive understanding of how and why employees are engaged. Creating ownership and accountability, and examining company culture from a more proactive point of view, must begin by correlating behavioral expectations with outcomes. *This is achieved by measuring how your leaders engage with employees within the organization and the specific effect these engagements have on driving positive business results.*

Then, by establishing visibility, when leaders fail to exhibit the behaviors that align with your company values (and the implications of these failures), proactive action is prompted to address them.

Understand, a proactive culture requires continuous reinforcements and role-modeling from the leadership team. Senior leaders must ensure the frontline leaders are engaged in actively promoting the desired company culture—they should show them the impact the values, behaviors, and interactions have on performance.

Proactively managing and measuring the results of your company culture is not a one-time initiative. It is an ongoing journey and needs steering.

PROBLEM #2: IS YOUR CULTURE PERFORMANCE MANAGEMENT EXECUTION ALIGNED?

Effective culture performance management requires perpetual refinement. We aren't trying to infer there's an ideological cultural state—but there *is* a system that helps you select your values, define them, connect, learn, and practice them, and then measure and refine them. Cultural performance management is designed to help all organizations, across every vertical, with *any* value set.

If everyone working in silos is important to your business, we can debate whether or not it's effective, but the system can best support you regardless. Every organization is going to have a different culture and whatever is important to you in an individual cultural value system should be perpetuated. We aren't advocating specific skills or competencies, rather alignment in the execution.

When the company hasn't defined its core values or the behaviors that align with those values, or taught their employees how to best execute those values, frontline employees have to figure it out on their own. Everyone defines things differently, but it's up to the company to level-set on those definitions with their employees.

Inconsistency happens when everyone brings their own value definitions to the table. Organizations expect all their employees to have the *same* definition, even when it hasn't been outlined explicitly, and behave the *same*, even when that hasn't been taught. But if the culture is misaligned (how could it not be?), is that really the fault of the employees? They want to do a good job, but how can they when they don't know what the organization's values are or how they're expected to behave?

We've worked with some very big US companies that don't define their company culture to the level they need to.

Big US Company: "We have values, but we're going to let the plant supervisors come up with their own definitions for the employees."

Us: "Why?"

Big US Company: "Because we don't want to micromanage them. We want them to have creative freedom to manage their culture as they see fit."

Us: "That's confusing for the other frontline leaders and employees though, because it's both prescriptive and *non*prescriptive."

Big US Company: "What do you mean by that?"

Us: "You're giving them a set of values you expect them to abide by, but you won't standardize the definitions or tell them how to incorporate those values into their daily workplace behaviors."

Consistency is king when values and behaviors are involved—organizations need to be prescriptive throughout the employees' journey. Having a process to manage your culture doesn't mean your leaders' unique interpersonal skills, abilities, and communication style have to change. Just because you have a construct around how you expect leaders to behave, interact, and engage doesn't mean you disable their creativity or individual leadership style.

TECHNICAL VERSUS TACTICAL

When business leaders think about skills and competency development, the *technical* components are typically front and center, but culture performance management is about the process, not the individual, and focuses on *tactical* execution. It explains the how and why (not the what and when) behind what leaders are doing hour over hour, day after day. It gives their work life direction.

One of the biggest complaints we get is this:

> If I standardize behaviors, my supervisors, frontline leaders, and employees will act like robots.

We understand this fear, but there is freedom in discipline. When there are rules to follow or parameters to stay between, it's *easier* to make decisions because there is less to choose from.

Think about going out to a restaurant. Is it easy to pick out your dinner when there are thirty menu pages to review? No! It will take you fifteen minutes just to read through it.

When you only have a handful of entrees to choose from, the process is simple and doesn't take very long. It's also less stressful. ("Do I order the Philly cheesesteak sandwich, the chicken parmesan, the seared ahi tuna, or the ribs? Argh! I can't decide!")

Standardizing behavior is a lot like that. When frontline leaders know how to act and behave at work, they're less stressed and mentally free to focus on their jobs. They can become more engaged at work.

PROBLEM #3: THE TALENT ACQUISITION AND RETENTION DEBACLE

Talent acquisition and retention is a big problem for executive leadership across all industries. Current market conditions perpetuated by our institutions (like SaaS, artificial intelligence, and machine learning), and most recently the COVID-19 virus, have created a talent shortage in the market. There aren't enough qualified candidates for most of the positions organizations need to fill.

The working population is changing, too. Baby boomers (generally, anyone born between 1946 and 1964) are retiring, so it's shifting to a millennial (1981–1996) and Gen Z (1997–2010) dominated environment. What these groups desire and value, and their interests and motivators, are different. For example, Gen Z is less interested in earning potential and job titles than they are in how an organization's culture will impact their experience while they work there. Does working for the company have a purpose? Gen Z isn't economically driven, it's purpose-driven.

An organization's ability to not only articulate the culture that exists in their business but measure and express how that culture impacts business *and* influences the employee experience should be critical to its recruitment strategy. The employee experience and a purpose-driven opportunity rank higher than earning potential, because people want to work for a company that shares their values.

Patagonia recently announced it will no longer sell its goods to Jackson Hole Ski Resort, their largest retailer in the area, because one of the resort owners recently hosted a fundraiser for the House Freedom Caucus, a conservative organization. This move will likely attract talent that shares its political values and repel those who don't.

Regardless of how you feel about the decision-making process of today's candidates, you have to understand where we currently are in the economic cycle. It is a buyers' market—they can pick and choose which company to work for based on its values. This is a result of a booming economy. If that changes, so does the behavior.

Because today's candidates are purpose-driven and focused on company values, companies need a system to define, practice, and measure the behaviors that align with their desired culture. They need to not only select values that align with their mission, the associated behaviors must be defined, too. Candidates want proof a company practices the culture it espouses, and this is only possible through Culture Performance Management.

PROBLEM #4: IS YOUR CULTURE PERFORMANCE MANAGEMENT LIKE QA OR QC?

Your current approach to develop and deliver on your company culture influences engagement, as well. Is it more aligned to the quality assurance (QA) or the quality control (QC) process? Knowing the answer to this question will illuminate options for you to consider when implementing and improving your desired company culture.

We aren't saying one of these quality processes is better than the other. Both QA and QC have the potential to add value. We are saying they are different.

- It is your choice to determine which quality process is more like your current approach in leading and implementing your cultural leadership behaviors.
- It is then your choice to determine which process best delivers on the cultural and operational performance outcomes you seek.
- Finally, it is your leadership responsibility to implement this process to achieve real cultural integrity (we act according to our values).

Let us frame up your thinking here with this truth: the inputs from your cultural processes determine the outcomes. We consider your employee experiences to be the outcome, or result, of your leadership behaviors, interactions, and management process.

Let's start with a comparison between QA and QC:

Quality Control and Quality Assurance Comparison Chart

QA	QC
A managing tool	A corrective tool
Process-oriented	Product-oriented
Proactive strategy	Reactive strategy
Prevention of defects	Detection of defects
Everyone's responsibility	Testing team's responsibility
Performed in parallel with a project	Performed after the final product is ready

By Sam Solutions

Now let us take these QA and QC "lenses" and look to see which quality approach aligns to your current cultural performance improvement process.

MANAGEMENT OR CORRECTIVE TOOL

In manufacturing and service organizations, a management tool is used throughout production to confirm, in real time, the right inputs are happening the right way and at the right time.

A cultural management tool assures that leader and employee behaviors, communications, and interactions align 100 percent with the company's cultural values and behaviors. High-quality management and leadership inputs lead to a quality employee experience outcome.

We are in favor of a management tool.

A corrective cultural tool is used to measure quality after the fact, after the leadership behaviors and interactions have produced the employee experience. The data from these surveys and pulsing is gathered, sorted, analyzed, and then used to figure out adjustments and actions to take to improve the leadership behaviors and interactions.

PROCESS-ORIENTED OR PRODUCT-ORIENTED

A process-oriented culture performance management approach is focused on making sure the right values, behaviors, skills, and interactions are built into each step of your process for facilitating your business. They are known and demonstrated by the leadership team in all they say and do.

A product-oriented culture performance management process focuses on the attitudes and opinions of the employees. It is the employees' evaluation of your leadership team that determines whether your leadership team is effective or not culturally based on the personal experiences of these employees.

DEFECT PREVENTION OR DEFECT DETECTION

Prevention of defects within a culture performance management system means the leaders are making sure the defective, or less than desirable, leadership behaviors and interactions do not happen in the first place. They make sure the ineffective leadership behaviors and interactions are removed, or reduced, before making their way into the employee experience.

Detection of defects within a culture performance management system uses the employees' opinions, feelings, and emotions as the defect test. If the employee engagement score is low, then it is inferred that the management behaviors and interactions need to be adjusted to make sure each employees' opinions, feelings, and emotions are satisfied.

WHO IS RESPONSIBLE?

If your cultural development, measurement, data gathering and improvement efforts reside within each teams' daily collective efforts, then your cultural improvement methods are everyone's responsibility, like QA.

If your cultural development, measurement, data gathering and improvement efforts reside within the human resources group then it is their responsibility to facilitate these processes, like QC.

PARALLEL OR POST-PRODUCT PERFORMANCE

Culture performance management processes that are woven and intertwined into the daily/weekly management operating system for executing the business lead to culture performed in parallel with all other management activities.

If your culture performance management process begins after the daily/weekly management operating system for executing your business with your teams, then your culture process is performed after the final product is ready, after the employee experiences the outcomes from the leadership behaviors and interactions.

Now that you have considered the two quality approaches of QA and QC, which cultural quality process is your company using?

Does your company have more of a cultural assurance process, more aligned to QA? Or, does your company have more of a cultural control process, more aligned to QC?

A HIGHLY RESPONSIVE PROCESS

QC is all about control, whereas QA is more flexible and more amenable to an environment that is constantly changing. That's why a cultural assurance process is more sustainable.

In today's ever-changing world, you have to create a process that is highly interactive, responsive to outcomes, and comprehendible. It also has to be specific and applied in real time. By its very nature, QC can't achieve this, because it's a process that takes place after the fact. QC is reactive and technical in nature, whereas QA is *pro*active and *tacti*cal.

PROBLEM #5: DOES YOUR COMPANY HAVE CULTURAL CREDIBILITY?

When an organization lives up to the company culture it espouses, it becomes credible. This is difficult to do if a culture performance management system is reactive and technical. Credible company culture can be established quickly but requires proactive, tactical management.

> **Cultural Credibility:** *The degree to which an organization lives up to its desired company culture as perceived by its relationship to people, both internally (employees) and externally (clients, media, etc.).*

Think about trial law and credible witnesses. They're credible because they are upstanding citizens and have a long, positive work history. Typically, credible witnesses have never been convicted of a crime. Moreover, the ultimate test of a witness's credibility is in the cross-examination—when the witness's statements (claims) are tested by the defense (the "outsiders" looking in, like your prospective employees, customers, suppliers, vendors, etc.). The greatest question posed to a witness to validate their credibility is the reliability of what they claim as true.

Is what you claim your company culture to be rooted in truth? Is it unimpeachable?

Credibility equates to trust. When you have cultural credibility, your employees and vendors all trust you to behave exactly as your values indicate. In other words, values that are backed by observable, verifiable behaviors and that match the expectations of frontline employees, managers, and vendors, establish credibility. It means you talk the talk *and* walk the walk.

Cultural credibility perpetuates trust and your believability. Not only do you speak your values, you deeply understand and *practice* them. For example, there are a lot of people who can quote religious scripture because they know it like the back of their hand, but do they *actually* live up to the values they're quoting? Credibility isn't just about speaking your values and adopting them into your everyday language; it's about embodying them to instill trust and dependability. You have been deemed a reliable source to articulate the values and demonstrate them accurately and consistently.

Every culture is different and there is no right or wrong way to manage it. You can choose what works best for your particular, unique business. A robust and consistent workplace culture that drives ideal outcomes takes hard, deliberate work and a strong understanding of values and how those play out at all levels, from the shop floor to the C-suite. Company culture impacts everyone.

PROBLEM #6: ARE YOU IN CULTURAL CHAOS?

Company culture impacts everyone in the organization; however, there are two points of convergence in a business where the viewpoints of leadership don't always align: operations and human resources. Sometimes their perspectives are unique and sometimes they overlap. Historically, because of the lack of a methodology and system to accurately define, manage, and optimize company culture, operations leaders tend to look to HR for solutions to their company culture problems.

From an HR perspective, breakdowns in company culture typically result in increased employee attrition and difficult talent acquisition. Oftentimes when company culture is addressed, employee turnover slows down and recruiting picks back up.

Generally speaking, operations leaders care about company culture because they've begun to recognize that frontline leaders play an integral role in day-to-day business execution. Frontline leadership culture should be an extension of company culture, because frontline leaders have a ripple effect on the entire frontline workforce. They are either contributing to the bottlenecks or fixing them.

For many frontline leaders, the employees' perception of engagement is secondary to their actual productivity. They ask what they can do to maximize the productivity of their frontline employees.

Ownership and adoption of your company culture begins with your frontline leaders. Failure to achieve the level of buy-in to your company culture vision and associated practices often relates to bottlenecks in your approach to communicating this vision. Educating them ensures they adopt a clear and aligned understanding of how your company values must be demonstrated through specific behaviors and interactions.

At the end of the day, company culture impacts operational performance and the organization's bottom line, so there must be a mechanism to measure it. Cultural performance should be viewed as an important strategic pillar for every business.

Despite good intentions, counterintuitive and counterproductive behavior around company culture persists, even when organizational values statements and corporate social responsibility are at the forefront of many consumer, economic, and commercial discussions.

This can create severe issues down the line, like employee retention, scalability, and profitability. Cultural chaos happens when values and acceptable behaviors aren't defined and predictable.

Cultural Chaos: *When a company has a set of values but hasn't standardized the definitions of those values, acceptable behavior cannot be established and taught. The result is behavioral disarray and bedlam.*

When value definitions aren't standardized, frontline leaders and employees don't know how to act. They become confused and disengaged.

Disengaged employees are costing companies billions, but the current methods of measuring culture and improving it aren't working; they don't connect to how frontline leaders practice the values and behaviors that embody the desired company culture. Only real-time *actual* behavioral data can have an immediate impact on company culture. Perceived behavioral data isn't as valuable.

If your organization is in a state of cultural chaos, you're in need of a quick fix—you don't have time to implement the full system just yet. You need help *right now* and need to see immediate results. Chapter 4, "How to Perform Cultural CPR," is up next.

CASE STUDY: DO YOU RECOGNIZE AND APPRECIATE YOUR EMPLOYEES?

Back in 2012, one of our clients (a food manufacturer of popular snack products) was experiencing challenges with high turnover and decided to embark on a big engagement survey initiative.

The company was making investments in their culture, but attrition was slowly increasing among its frontline leaders and employees. So, executive management wanted to find a methodology to gauge employee engagement and determine what skills were needed to enhance the employee experience.

We looked at data from more than thirty-eight plants and discovered their engagement score hadn't moved—it was stagnant. Digging in deeper, the story was the same—it all came down to leadership behavior.

We wanted to understand their leadership culture, but from their perspective. What did they see as their strengths and weaknesses? What were their opportunities and threats? Those were the internal catalysts either lifting them up and getting them closer to their desired leadership culture or keeping them from achieving it.

Through that exercise, we found their perception of their behaviors was different from the employees' perceptions. Leaders believed they were recognizing and appreciating their employees, for example, but survey data from their teams said otherwise.

"We want to be recognized."

"We want to be appreciated."

"We want more investment in us as employees."

With this new information, our client decided to change things up. They asked their employees what they valued, and investments in employee events and wage and pay equity were made; they also put money into additional training opportunities. Attrition decreased and employee engagement increased.

PART 2

CULTURE PERFORMANCE MANAGEMENT

CHAPTER 4

———

DOES YOUR COMPANY CULTURE NEED CPR?

Back in 2011, actress Kate Winslet saved the life of Richard Branson's mother. Yes. In real life.

(In case you've been living under a rock, Branson is a billionaire investor and founder of the Virgin Group. You may better recognize him as the "Virgin Airlines Guy.")

Winslet and her family were vacationing with Branson and *his* family at his private island home in the British Virgin Islands when it caught fire and burned to the ground. Twenty people were inside when the fire started, including Branson's ninety-year-old mom. They all made it out alive, thanks to Winslet, who carried Branson's mom out of the house to safety. She was quick to react in an emergency—she was mentally prepared.

Emergency responsiveness is a specialized skill, one that requires classroom *and* field training. For example, nurses, doctors, healthcare providers (and police officers, firefighters, and other rescue personnel) are typically trained in CPR, an emergency lifesaving technique that uses chest compressions and rescue breaths if some-one's heart has stopped or they aren't breathing.

How does this all relate to company culture?

Many business leaders realize their company culture is dead or on life support. Values may exist in theory or concept; however, leadership behaviors and interactions are misaligned with the company's values.

If this rings true for you, and you need to breathe new life into your company culture—it's time to perform cultural CPR.

WHAT IS CULTURAL CPR?

The cultural CPR process is a comprehensive and straightforward formula to revive your company culture as a first step in realizing its full potential. Before you can "operationalize" your company culture with the implementation of a culture performance management system, you must first awaken your leaders to ensure they are prepared to take all the necessary steps toward cultivating, fostering, and protecting your desired company culture—one that is consistent with your organization's values and belief system.

Some organizations need CPR before they can begin to discuss the logistics of the major company culture surgery. They need CPR to first stabilize their culture performance management. After that, the CPM system can be applied.

Simply put, CPR stands for:

CPR = Consciousness + Practice + Results

Now that you are familiar with the formula, let's dive into the details of each uniquely crucial component of cultural CPR.

C = CREATE CULTURAL CONSCIOUSNESS

You cannot expect your workforce to understand the core values and principles you believe should influence their behaviors (and guide your business) unless you teach and model them. This level of awareness and understanding of your values within your organization is cultural consciousness.

Cultural Consciousness: *The state of being awake and aware of one's organizational culture, emphasizing the values that shape the behaviors and interactions between individuals within an organization.*

Effective communication is at the root of any teaching and learning process. You must integrate your company values and behaviors purposefully and consistently in your organizational conversations. Furthermore, you must include the benefits of a robust culture in the ongoing discussion with your team. When they understand how the organization's values and beliefs impact their own work experience, they will become more accountable for the behaviors and interactions that embody a stronger culture.

While "overmarketizing" your company culture can appear disingenuous, to create cultural consciousness, your company values, belief statements, and standards of behavior should be documented and shared throughout your organization. Meetings should begin and end with thoughts on what you believe as an organization or how employees exhibit core values critical to your organization's success. The intrinsic value of your culture should be talked about, discussed, and emphasized.

To assess your organization's cultural consciousness, ask yourself these ten questions:

1. Is developing your company culture part of your daily work?
2. Do your or your team's actions reflect your company's cultural values?
3. Is the strength of your culture profoundly crucial to you or your organization?
4. Have you consistently made your culture a priority?
5. Can members of your team (including frontline employees) state your company values?
6. If you ask five members of your team to explain what your company values mean, would you get an accurate definition?
7. If you ask five members of your team to explain what your company values mean, would you get a consistent definition?
8. Are the behaviors associated with your company's values clearly defined?
9. Do you, or members of your team, understand the behaviors that represent the values that serve as the foundation of your company culture?
10. Have you communicated expectations regarding these behaviors and associated interactions that influence your company culture?

If you answered "no" to two or more questions, your cultural consciousness is likely slipping. Take the proper steps to ensure every member of your team recognizes and acknowledges the defined values that *must* shape their behaviors and interactions, between themselves and others, within your organization.

P = PROMOTE DAILY PRACTICE

You are an organizational leader, so people within your business look to you as an example of how to behave and interact with others. Moreover, you and your entire leadership team set the standard for what is considered acceptable behavior. It's that simple—they look at what you do and listen to what you say. They take all your actions into account and then—consciously or subconsciously—decide whether you demonstrate leadership integrity.

Some well-intentioned companies will go as far as establishing, defining, and even communicating their organizational values, detailing how to behave and interact with one another. However, these organizations have failed in "operationalizing" or practicing these values or, in other words, fostering the learning of core values and behaviors that lead to optimal business performance by way of better engagement. Practicing company culture requires daily education, observation, and rehearsal to improve how individuals interact with one another when performing throughout the day. It requires discipline and commitment. A simple method for practicing your culture every day is to teach, assess, and repeat.

You don't need a lot of content to provide clear, concise, specific, and actionable training. The goal here is to produce effective training material that sticks, and *quickly.* You're in lifesaving, CPR mode, and too much content tends to:

- Take too long to create or
- Be counterproductive to what you're trying to achieve, which is information retention.

Learning and retention happen in three stages: early stage, middle stage, and late stage.

1. *Early-stage learning* refers to the period of development when

the adult learner is attempting to grasp the fundamental principles and concepts they're taught. During this phase of learning, the emphasis should be to foster the learner's comprehension and adoption of the language and how this applies to one's understanding and connection to action. This aligns with what we consider to be the "mechanical" phase of adoption, compliance, and retention.

2. *Middle-stage learning* refers to the period of development when the adult learner has grasped the fundamental principles and concepts taught, and is now focused on practical application. During this phase of learning, the emphasis should be to foster the learner's conceptual understanding of why these principles and concepts are important and how the application of these learned practices impacts outcomes (consequences). This aligns with what we consider to be the "conceptual" phase of adoption, compliance, and retention.

3. *Late-stage learning* refers to the period of development when the adult learner exhibits complete understanding of the fundamental principles and concepts taught, but has also adopted the supporting behavioral practices and awareness of the cause-effect relationship between one's actions and the results as they relate to these practices. During this phase of learning, the emphasis should be to foster the learner's empowerment to promote continuous improvement, advanced learning, and application. This aligns with what we consider to be the "ownership" phase of adoption, compliance, and retention.

We're trying to generate the greatest amount of retention through awareness and initial interest, all the way through to evaluation, application, and connection. When there is purpose behind learning, retention increases, and when information is concise, clear, and direct, retention is even higher. From a culture performance management perspective, that means explicitly defining acceptable behaviors and standards for engagement and identifying connection points in leaders' day-to-day interactions.

(Here's a quick tip: the most incredible retention rates are typically seen in digital platform learning and short, to-the-point bite-size videos and audio clips.)

Classroom-style learning has the lowest retention because it's much harder to comprehend and retain all that information at once. It's how children have always been taught in school, but even that system has seen innovation in recent decades with the emergence of charter schools—students needed a different way to learn.

Frontline leaders have many distractions to deal with because they work in a fast-paced, complex environment. They need an adaptive learning model because it increases the probability of practicing the organization's defined behaviors and embodying its culture.

Different learner types need to be considered, too. Visual learners need to see what they're learning, so reading and writing work well for them. Lectures and podcasts are suitable for auditory learners—videos work well for both. Kinesthetic learners need discussion and practice. Knowing how to teach others means understanding how they learn.

Step 1: Teach Your Team to Embody Your Culture

Teaching your employees how to behave in alignment with the company's culture begins by confirming their understanding and recognition of a simple truth: their interactions with each other are the embodiment of your company's values and are paramount to improve how they engage with each other and performance outcomes for the business. This critical learning outcome provides clear examples of how specific communication approaches promote and encourage or detract from certain behaviors, thus positively or negatively impacting results.

For instance, let's say your organization values commitment. The traits of dedication, resolve, decisiveness, and attentiveness are behaviors that exemplify that value. When you model these traits, you guide your team leaders in their daily interactions and teach them how to embody that value. You may provide even simpler examples like showing up to critical meetings on time and consistently, demonstrating respect for clients and colleagues.

This example is a direct reflection of how a person shows dedication to a deemed essential process. Furthermore, these behaviors reflect a level of attentiveness to the individuals asked to participate in that process.

Step 2: Assess Your Team's Interactions

Assessment of how individuals interact with one another is critical to practicing your company culture. The level at which their behavior and interactions align with company values provides a benchmark to measure future improvement. Typical employee assessments provide lagging information; to assess and improve your culture, you need real-time information and action. A real-time evaluation will show that individuals within your organization recognize how their behaviors and interactions successfully (or unsuccessfully) align with the culture you are working to foster.

For example, you may schedule time, twice per day, to observe how they engage with their front-line employees. During this observation, evaluate how their actions and decision-making align with and support the company's value system.

During your assessment of how your leaders behave and interact with one another, you will want to answer the following:

1. Did the interactions between your leaders and employees exemplify your core company values?
2. Was there an apparent awareness of the company value system that informed how individuals interacted with one another?
3. Were there direct or indirect references to the company values, beliefs, or associated behaviors during the interactions?
4. Did your employees reciprocate or emulate the appropriate practices that are indicative of your company value system?
5. When faced with a challenge, did you observe your leaders' application of your company value system as part of their decision-making process?

Findings from your leadership interactions assessment should provide you with insights on additional developmental opportunities for your team. For example, answering "no" to Question 4: is a clear indicator that the behavioral practices of your leaders have not translated to your employees in a manner that would impact their own behaviors over time. This may be due to a lack of engaged interaction with their leaders or an inability to recognize the connection between what's observed from their leaders and what's expected of themselves behaviorally.

Considering this point, the guidance you provide the leaders should include how they use their own actions, or the actions of their peers, as examples when explaining how they expect their employees to behave acceptably and embody the company values. Furthermore, the leaders could be guided to become more intentional and deliberate in their use of the language surrounding the company values and associated behavioral practices. This includes immediate acknowledgement and celebration when a leader observes the appropriate behaviors from their employees and corrective action when the counter-behaviors are identified.

Step 3: Repeat, Then Repeat Again

Once insights are in hand, this step intends that *everyone* work to realize a company culture that fulfills the organization's mission, vision, and purpose. Applying these considerations to the feedback provided to everyone in the organization, to discuss areas of opportunity and offer insights, warrants a repeat of the process.

Practicing culture is a never-ending process of self-reflection, education, feedback, and application. It is a journey that will significantly improve employee experiences and overall productivity.

R = RESULTS

Creating ownership and accountability surrounding your company culture must begin with correlating behavioral expectations of your frontline leaders with outcomes. You achieve this by measuring how they engage with employees within the organization (the results from the assessment in Step 2 of P) and the specific effect on driving positive business results.

By establishing visibility around a leader's failure to exhibit the behaviors that align with your company values, and the implications of these failures, you prompt proactive action to address them. Leaders will need to "step up." The same applies to identifying positive leadership behaviors and practices that align with your company's values.

Indicators to consider when measuring the results of your cultural practices:

1. Has the frequency and quality of the interactions between leaders and employees changed? For example, has it improved?
2. Has the quality of your leaders' decision-making improved? For instance, did the leadership address the root cause of issues?
3. Has your frontline team's productivity shifted in alignment with the change in the level of leadership engagement, either positively or negatively?

Measuring cultural performance management outcomes and the impact that these outcomes have on your business requires a correlation to specific performance indicators. When measuring results of your cultural performance, consider the tangible and intangible variables influenced by your leader's behaviors and interactions—including productivity, employee or client retention, sales acquisitions, safety incidences, employee engagement scores, and more.

Making the connection between your company's culture performance, and the result of the leadership behaviors you have emphasized, is not an easy task. Many business leaders struggle with making these connections because they have not correlated behavioral practices tangibly for their business. While we will explore this further later in the book, let's talk dollars and cents for a moment ("Show Me the Money!").

Culture Performance Management Impact

Behavioral Ownership & Accountability

People-Centered Tactical Interactions

Improved Talent Retention

Improved Cost Management

Improved Awareness of Performance

Increased Leadership Engagement

Increased Skills & Competencies

Increased Skills Flexibility

Reduced New-Hire "Learning Curve"

Consistent Leadership Training

Increased Staffing Fulfillment

Reduced Turnover & Attrition

Process/System-Centered Technical Interaction

Reduced Excess Labor Costs

Reduced Unplanned OT

Reduced HR Ops. Expense

Reduced Hiring Costs

Increased Capacity

Reduced Waste (All Categories)

Increased Throughput

Increased Productivity

Reduced Time to Market

Improved Quality

Increased Margins

A leader's ownership of the behaviors that you have deemed most critical to realizing your company culture is directly related to how stakeholders are engaged and decisions are made. This makes finding the connection to financial outcomes easier.

The bottom line is, when your leaders foster stronger technical and tactical interactions, it will have a ripple effect on the people-centered functions of your business, as noted in the diagram (working from the left, bottom to top, or on the right, bottom to top). Reduction in labor costs, operation expenses, and waste in your business impacts your P&L, as do increases in productivity, quality, throughput, and capacity.

In your business, these changes are only possible because of how leaders engage, interact, and make decisions that improve how talent is acquired, retained, developed, and managed.

A TIME FOR CHANGE

You're probably used to seeing headlines featured in *Forbes, Entrepreneur, Business Insider*, and others, declaring the "Twenty-five companies with the best culture" or "Fifteen places with the best work-life balance." Company culture and everything it comprises—the vision, values, norms, systems, symbols, language, assumptions, beliefs, and habits at the workplace—has gained a great deal of traction in recent years.

It's not only a favorite area of coverage for business reporters but also a trendy discussion item at major conferences and seminars—company culture can both engage employees and bolster productivity, leading to increased profits.

By now, it should be clear that most organizations approach their company cultures ineffectively because they have misrepresented their values, have not actively defined their acceptable behaviors, or aren't actively practicing them. These actions (or nonactions) have created a disingenuous culture—it lacks integrity.

For some organizations, this realization needs an emergency fix, a.k.a. cultural CPR. What would have happened to Richard Branson's mom if Kate Winslet wasn't mentally (and physically) prepared?

Other companies are ready for the next step: culture performance management. Once this reality has been accepted, **the next step is to do something about it.**

However, if you still aren't convinced you need a cultural performance management system, it's time to put this book down. The rest revolves around active steps that will improve how company culture is defined, managed, and measured.

Accepting reality means facing the undeniable. If you're having trouble with talent acquisition and retention and your employee experience scores haven't moved in ten years, you aren't effectively managing your company culture.

Behavioral change requires a conscious acceptance of the circumstances. Anyone who wants to improve their company culture must first consciously accept that their culture needs improvement. Then, they have to have a strong desire and readiness to do what's necessary to improve it.

Accepting reality is a prerequisite for taking action.

If you're having a hard time accepting the truth about your company culture, you're not alone. Most of the executive leaders we talk to about their cultures aren't easily convinced. We typically spend four to five days assessing their cultures and showing them inefficiencies until they are finally beaten into submission.

"Okay! Okay! You're right. Our culture needs help. Let's get started!"

The CPM system is coming up next.

CHAPTER 5

CULTURE PERFORMANCE MANAGEMENT

Parkfield, California, is the earthquake capital of the world. It's located in Monterey County along the San Andreas Fault and is the world's most closely observed earthquake zone. Every twenty-two years historically, a 6.0 magnitude earthquake has happened there.[4]

Structural engineers are among the people who study earthquakes and have figured out ways to make buildings safer. Some of their designs include:

- Flexible buildings that can rock back and forth without cracking,
- *Tuned mass dampers*, which are heavy weights placed at the top of very tall buildings to help counter vibrations from an earthquake, and
- Isolation bearings that allow the base of a building to move

---

4   "Parkfield," SeeMonterey.com, accessed July 5, 2021, https://www.seemonterey.com/regions/parkfield/#:~:text=Known%20as%20the%20%22Earthquake%20Capital,has%20occurred%20every%2022%20years.

with the quake, but keep its main structure in place, sort of like shock absorbers on a car.[5]

When these ideas were first introduced, they were brilliant, but in order to be implemented, the buildings needed to be sound. For example, how can a flexible structure be built upon a wobbly foundation?

Design and structure are *both* important. Before any of these ideas could come to fruition, engineers had to plan and shape them. Without a sound foundation that has been carefully thought out and meticulously constructed, the building won't be able to carry out its purpose: to remain upright during an earthquake.

Your company culture is no different. It needs a strategic design and meticulous structure. It needs culture performance management.

(We first defined culture performance management in the beginning of the book, but it's been a while. So, here it is again.)

Culture Performance Management (CPM): *Culture performance management refers to the system for aligning an organization's core company values, with specific and actionable leadership behaviors that can be practiced, evaluated, and measured in real time, in order to drive immediate improvement in how leaders engage, interact, and make decisions. The ultimate objective is to foster short-interval and continuous improvement of one's company culture. This is achieved through the implementation of a comprehensive CPM that connects leadership engagement and work execution touchpoints that ultimately influence business performance outcomes. CPM is designed to support the sustainability of performance results. It also provides visibility into the progress leaders make toward practicing the behaviors that serve as an ideal company culture requisite.*

---

5 Ben Finio, "Earthquake Rollers," *Scientific American*, April 20, 2017, https://www. scientificamerican.com/article/earthquake-rollers/.

CPM is a robust process that allows business executives to evaluate and measure frontline leaders' behaviors daily, provide feedback for continuous development, and align and lead an ideal company culture. The CPM system is designed to support the sustainability of performance results, which includes KPIs and engagement scores. These provide visibility into the progress specific leaders are making practicing the behaviors that serve as a requisite to support the ideal company culture.

THE SYSTEM

Culture performance management establishes an empirical and results-driven approach for how the organization routinely and systematically defines, communicates, and measures its company culture. It's a system that combines seven pillars representing the foundational and consecutive steps an organization must take to operationalize their desired practice; CPM moves them from ideological "window dressing" concepts to a real, practical, and experiential company culture.

The seven pillars of a CPM system are:

- Pillar #1: Select
- Pillar #2: Define
- Pillar #3: Connect
- Pillar #4: Learn
- Pillar #5: Practice
- Pillar #6: Measure
- Pillar #7: Refine

A CPM is designed to complement and integrate with most management operating systems (MOS) within an organization. By leveraging a series of interrelated systems, processes, and associated tools that enable leaders to execute the business through a technical lens, an MOS refers to an operational framework for work execution in any business. However, a CPM system aligns more closely with how leaders examine and optimize the business through a more tactical lens; i.e., understanding the connection between leadership behaviors and how they impact employee engagement, interactions, and decision-making. When implementing a CPM system, business leaders are required to consider the following:

- Why are leaders behaving the way they are?
- How do they communicate with their direct reports?
- Why did they make that decision?
- How do they engage and interact with their colleagues, peers, customers, and stakeholders?
- How do my leaders establish trust, respect, and equality?

Overlapping an MOS with a CPM system creates an optimal operational culture, because all standards of leadership behavior that maximize performance are defined, communicated, and managed in a manner that establishes predictability and scale in business. When only the systems and processes behind the executed work are examined, the impact is minimized because there is limited consideration regarding *how* leaders are *actually* leveraging these tools to engage with employees while making critical decisions for the business. It's a full, 360-degree view of your operational culture—centered on the organization's value system and behavioral standards as the catalyst to realizing the full potential of the business.

UNDERSTANDING WHY CULTURE PERFORMANCE MANAGEMENT IS ESSENTIAL

We recognize that most organizations want culture performance management. They recognize "culture" impacts their business performance, but it's through a lens often blurred by misperceptions, rhetoric, or market pressures. The CPM system provides a solution, but first, leaders must understand company culture as a construct before they can develop and implement a system to manage it. This is the first proactive and aligned method or approach to measuring, managing, and improving the leadership behaviors producing the company's culture, in real time. This system enables leaders to take sequential and integral steps to implement and sustain the company culture they know to be critical to their success.

The seven pillars of our system are the essential elements of CPM. Like a building's foundation is paramount to its long-term success, your CPM ensures your company culture can be sustained and replicated over time. When a building is constructed, the foundation is laid first. Next comes the frame, followed by wiring the electric and installing the plumbing. All of these elements have to be done correctly to construct a sturdy building that will weather any storm. They're essential. In the same context, your CPM provides structure and an easy-to-follow framework that equips your frontline leaders with the confidence and tools to embody the organization's values, behaviors, and standards for engagement. The system is a blueprint of your company culture.

Our CPM system encourages the review of your cultural performance on the frontlines of your business, through the evaluation of manager and supervisor collaboration and feedback, on-the-job learning with customized educational resources, and developmental tracks. It connects frontline leaders and employees with the knowledge they need to fully embody the company culture.

As you begin to operationalize your company culture by way of the culture performance management system, it is important to understand the gaps between your current-state culture performance and desired future state.

WHERE DOES YOUR CULTURE LAND, OVERALL?

Many organizations will tell you their perception of their company culture is that it's healthy, both in terms of leadership engagement and employee experience. They believe the communication they've built around their value system and their improvements to their leadership culture have had a positive impact. However, their perceptions often differ from those of their employees, which is a problem.

When we talk with our clients about improving leadership culture, the conversation typically begins with a discussion about their observations and why they called us in the first place. We'll validate (or invalidate) those observations on our own, but we always start with personal acknowledgment, similar to the following conversation:

Us: "What have you observed of your company culture?"

Client: "I'm not getting the results I want from my leadership team."

Then, we'll dig deeper.

Us: "What does that mean? What exactly are the results you aren't getting?"

Their initial responses are typically technical.

Client: "I do not see the attainment rates I want."

This response is usually only skimming the surface of the issue, so we'll drill down even more. The client's problems *could* indicate a system or process breakdown; however, through dialogue we arrive at a point in the discussion when we begin to correlate system and process challenges with leadership behavior or skills competency gaps.

When it's system or process related, most business operators apply mechanisms to understand daily performance—they can evaluate and report on performance variance. However, when challenges are related to leadership behavior or skills competency challenges, leaders find it more difficult to articulate through an objective lens—especially when connecting how these challenges impact the business.

To help shift executive management's mindset on the implications of how their leaders' behaviors impact the business, we ask a series of questions to prompt dialogue:

- "Are our frontline leaders engaged with employees on the floor?"
- "What kind of conversations are they having?"
- "Does their behavior align with our company's core values?"

That dialogue typically reveals the potential for deeper-rooted leadership culture issues. It might be a lack of leadership competency, skills, behavioral understanding, or many other circumstances. Nonetheless, we immediately recommend an assessment of their culture; we leverage a series of diagnostic tools and best practices to assist us in validating perceived root-cause issues and reveal the truth behind the challenges that impact the business. Our objective behind this assessment is to provide our critique of the factors creating a gap between the business's current and desired leadership culture.

The good news is there are a few assessments you can explore to conduct your own cultural "gap" analysis.

Let's start with a *Cultural SWOT (Strengths, Weaknesses, Opportunities, and Threats) Analysis.*

ASSESSMENT: CULTURAL SWOT ANALYSIS

- **Definition:** Analysis of the strengths, weaknesses, opportunities, and threats facing the company that directly influence the leadership culture and performance outcomes.
- **Objective:** Leverage strengths, mitigate weaknesses, capitalize on opportunities, and minimize threats to the desired leadership culture.

When we think about climate, we think about the atmosphere and the physical environment. Perception is also considered— sixty-five degrees will feel cold to one person but comfortable to someone else.

What are the characteristics of the leadership culture that give it advantages over its competitors?

What are the characteristics that make it *dis*advantageous?

Are there elements of the company's external environment that allow for enhancements to the leadership culture?

Are there any that could compromise its integrity?

The SWOT Analysis is all about gauging the cultural climate.

> **Cultural Climate:** *The current "temperature" of organizational company culture at any given time assessed. It's how the workplace environment impacts the culture. Not the vision or the perception—it's what's actually happening.*

- Your cultural climate is based upon the perceived culture (at all levels) within a workplace versus the actual, measurable culture. What is the actual cultural "temperature" within your organization?
- And what are the implications of it?

Many organizations have a different perception of their culture than their employees do. They also fail to realize their cultural climate will typically ebb and flow. So, how do they get real feedback from both parties and measure it in real time?

The Cultural SWOT Analysis tool allows you to garner a collective perspective on an organization's current cultural climate—exploring the internal strengths and weaknesses contributing to it, as well as external opportunities and threats posed by consumers, competitors, and the general marketplace that may influence your company culture.

Are your leadership dynamics centered on trust? Are your values focused on integrity and inclusion? Regardless of the company values (Pillar #1: Select), measuring your cultural climate is about understanding the current state of your workplace environment and subsequent employee experience at all levels of the organization.

As part of your Cultural SWOT Analysis, you will want to explore your leaders' perspectives regarding how well they understand and exhibit the behaviors that align with your company's value system. You can do this using a Gap Analysis.

ASSESSMENT: GAP ANALYSIS

- **Definition:** Analysis of the current manager-to-employee interactions and decision points and processes that identify process and system opportunities and drive communication and engagement to influence company culture (missing information, redundancies, non-value-added activities, etc.).
- **Objective:** Highlight issues between systems, behaviors, and processes that drive when, where, and how leaders engage, interact, and make decisions.

The feedback and insights you collect through a Gap Analysis will help enable you to establish a *culture baseline* to measure against and determine the "gap" between your current- and ideal-state cultures.

When interactions between leaders and employees happen, is information missing?

Are non-value-added activities included in the exchange?

Are there redundancies in processes and communication between leaders and their teams?

Understanding the gaps will help you begin to identify the steps (the pillars) you need to take to help you achieve your desired company culture.

> **Cultural Baseline:** *Established behavioral strengths and weaknesses metrics from which you can train, evaluate, monitor, and improve the behaviors and attitudes of executive management and frontline leaders.*

A cultural baseline should include a quantifiable metric that is mathematically derived. To do that, we use a Gap Analysis to determine the state of a client's CPM system.

- Have they selected values?
- Are those values defined and have they been connected to acceptable values?
- Have frontline leaders and employees learned and practiced those values?
- Has executive management measured the demonstration of those values?
- What are they doing to refine those values and the behaviors associated with them?

The Gap Analysis measures a company's current culture-state against its ideal one. It is an evaluation of how well the observed leadership behaviors align and *mis*align with the core company values the organization has established.

(Note: This is more closely examined upon completion of the *Cultural Vision Alignment* assessment.)

LEAD AN IDEAL COMPANY CULTURE

Structural engineers have figured out how to build earthquake-proof buildings based on the way they want those buildings to behave. A building that bends and moves with the quake is less likely to break, so they figured out how to design and structure flexible ones.

Our prospective clients often state, "I expect my managers and frontline leaders to behave in a specific way, but I don't see it."

This thought process reflects the opportunity they have to advance their CPM. For each pillar of the CPM system, there are a series of assessments they can perform to begin to understand how to fill their cultural gaps.

CPM is a system that allows business executives to lead an ideal company culture. It is designed to sustain performance results.

Like those buildings, company culture needs both design *and* structure. It needs culture performance management.

It's time to explore the CPM pillars and accompanying assessments.

CHAPTER 6

PILLAR #1

SELECT

**Core-4™
Company
Value**

**Behaviors
that Embody
Company Values**

∨

**1
Select
(Value System)**

PowerPoint is a software program used to create slideshow presentations, or visual representations of information, to be shared with executives. It was created by Robert Gaskins and Dennis Hawkins (for a software company called Forethought, Inc.) and released on April 20, 1987. It was Microsoft Corporation's first major acquisition and was purchased for $14 million roughly three months after it was released.

In a broad context, the seven pillars of culture performance management were established to provide a simple and actionable visual representation for corporate executives, frontline leaders, and employees, similar to PowerPoint. The first pillar is Select, which refers to an organization's identification and selection of the core values that serve as the guiding principles and fundamental beliefs to inform how stakeholders must function together as a team and work toward a common business goal. Every CPM requires a foundational set of values that *all* employees are expected to embody when interacting with others and making decisions that impact the business.

It's rare, but sometimes we encounter clients who don't have company values defined at all. This isn't necessarily a bad thing, because it gives us the opportunity to facilitate the process of identifying these values with a clean slate. For these clients, we recommend working backwards and to start by identifying what performance success looks like and the driving factors behind it. We suggest they have an open discussion with their executive management team to help flush out what's important, from a leader-to-employee engagement and decision-making perspective. From there, underlying themes will start to surface and the values-selection process will be more straightforward and connect to what drives success within the business.

During the values-selection process, leaders should be careful about choosing values that don't align with their ideal cultural state. Organizations that haven't factored their idea of cultural success into their values-selection process will fail to create an explicitly defined values system. This will make it difficult for leaders to understand and meet the expectations of how one should engage and make decisions on behalf of the organization.

ASSESSMENTS: SELECT

Understanding begins with assessing. For Step 1: Select, we start with a *Cultural Vision Alignment* assessment to examine and explore how well the senior leadership team has developed, communicated, and aligned priorities in support of the organization's cultural vision. This requires an examination of the core values that are considered paramount to the organization's fulfillment of its mission, vision, and purpose. For organizations that don't have a value system selected, this may be the ideal opportunity to work through the exercise of determining or revisiting what their values should be.

ASSESSMENT: CULTURAL VISION ALIGNMENT

- **Definition:** A qualitative and quantitative diagnostic tool that examines the perspectives of an organization's senior leaders to determine how they perceive the company culture, as compared to the ideal-state culture.
- **Objective:** To understand if the current-state vision and supporting practices surrounding the operational culture align with senior organizational leaders' desired ideal-state company culture, identify disconnects in vision and practice, and reveal opportunities for better communication and clarity around cultural vision.

Do the operational practices align with executive management's ideal company culture?

Are frontline leaders and employees embodying the company's cultural vision? Are they practicing its acceptable behaviors?

What are the opportunities for better articulation of the company's values?

(Note: We have customized workshops and associated activities that enable senior leader teams to work through this sometimes complex exercise.)

Similarly, we also explore the organization's goals and strategies to determine to what extent these goals have been effectively communicated throughout the organization.

ASSESSMENT: GOALS AND STRATEGIES ALIGNMENT

- **Definition:** A quantitative diagnostic tool designed to measure the organization's alignment, regarding the goals and the strategies required to meet organizational performance objectives, between frontline leaders and their senior leadership team.
- **Objective:** To reveal the adequacy and efficacy of top-down communication throughout the organization.

Has executive management aligned with frontline leaders about their strategies to meet the company's goals?

Have executive management and frontline leadership ranked those goals in order of importance?

Has a visual representation of that information been created (and then presented) to aid in understanding?

Every organization should check in with their teams' understanding of its goals and strategies. Another benefit is that the examination of the results generated from the Cultural Vision

Alignment and Goals and Strategies Alignment assessments may begin to reveal the depth of your organization's cultural character.

> **Cultural Character:** *The "personality"/nature/temperament of a company's culture—the state of the stakeholder's mindset (attitudes and behaviors) as reflected within the work environment.*

What is your cultural character today? What do you want it to look like tomorrow?

What you do day-to-day as an organization defines your cultural character. It doesn't matter which plaques you have on the wall or which value systems you ascribe to; real character is visible through actions, interactions, and decision-making.

CHANGE FOR THE BETTER

This isn't about whether an organization's cultural character is positive or negative—the term is ideologically neutral in this context. When we talk about cultural character, we're referring to the attitudes and behaviors your leaders have toward the activities and challenges facing your company culture. The good news is, like the personal character of an individual, your cultural character can change for the better if you invest in the right action steps.

Your frontline leaders will evaluate your organization's cultural character by what you, as corporate management, say and do. Your frontline employees will do the same to their supervisors— the frontline leaders. And if these behaviors don't align with their definitions of the organization's values, they'll think ill of your cultural character and, thus your corporate culture.

PowerPoint presentations provide executives with the essential information they need to assess the situation and make a decision. Culture performance management provides executives with the essential information *they* need to determine whether or not company employees display the character that matches the organization's values. If a corporate executive is always an hour late to a monthly site visit, can their employees trust them to be *reliable*, one of the organization's values?

To take this even further, how do you think witnessing this behavior impacts the employees over time? They'll start to believe those are the workplace standards and that anyone who *doesn't* reciprocate that behavior will stick out like a sore thumb. Suddenly, *un*reliability is perpetuated at the operator level—through observation, they take on those behaviors. (This is called "social learning theory.")

All the more reason why a culture performance management system is needed to define culture, learn how to behave by it, and then measure it. Without this foundation, an organization's cultural character is at risk.

When selecting your values, you must bridge the gap between value-intent and value-practice. To make the connection, leaders must progress from selection and communication of the core values shaping one's future-state culture, to defining these values with specificity regarding the behaviors that individuals must practice to embody those values. Once the work has been done to establish the core values that are paramount to realizing or sustaining a positive workplace culture, leaders must transition from a broad and generalized understanding of what these values mean to a specific and actionable definition of how these values must be exhibited daily. It's time to move to Pillar #2 of the culture performance management system: Define.

CHAPTER 7

PILLAR #2

DEFINE

Core-4™
Company
Value

_____

Behaviors
that Embody
Company Values

∨

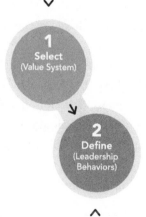

Behavioral
Expectations

_____

Standards for
Engagement

Merriam-Webster has four definitions for "dictionary":

1. A reference source in print or electronic form containing words usually alphabetically arranged along with information about their forms, pronunciations, functions, etymologies, meanings, and syntactic and idiomatic uses
2. A reference book listing alphabetically terms or names important to a particular subject or activity along with discussion of their meanings and applications
3. A reference book listing alphabetically the words of one language and showing their meanings or translations in another language
4. A computerized list (as of items of data or words) used for reference (as for information retrieval or word processing).

Dictionaries date all the way back to the Mesopotamian city of Elba in ancient Sumer (modern Syria) around 2300 BCE.[6] They have been around almost as long as humankind itself, so one could argue they have been instrumental in its modernization. Dictionaries provide definitions, which lead to common understanding.

Once you select your company's value system, the next step is to understand how you believe these values are paramount to your business success and the specific actions that foster positive outcomes for your organization. You do this by first clarifying your general definition for each value. For example, if your company value is *Innovation*, ensure you have a clear and concise definition of what it means, in general terms:

> To seek new ideas or enhancements to processes and products that improve how we serve our customers every day.

---

6   "Dictionary," *MSN Encarta*, accessed September 12, 2021, https://web.archive.org/web/20091029091932/http://encarta.msn.com/encyclopedia_761573731/Dictionary.html.

It's time to get specific after you have clarified your general definition for your company values. More than simply defining the value, you have to make the value definition *actionable*—it needs to include specific behavioral expectations that can be practiced at every level of the organization.

For example:

- Does the value of innovation, as defined, mean presenting solutions in tandem with problems?
- Does it require an interest in continuous improvement??
- Does it mean that in our daily interactions and follow-ups we expect leaders to ask employees their thoughts and ideas regarding how the process can be improved?

When defining the behavioral expectations underpinning your company values, you must be specific, so it's clear how you expect frontline leaders and employees to behave. Be clear and unwavering about the exact behaviors that leaders must embody to represent your company values. For example, consider the value of *Innovation* as previously defined. A more concise definition may include the following language:

> Our Innovative team members are observant, aware, encouraging, and bold: they always seek out, solicit, and share methods to improve how we serve our customers quicker, faster, and with better quality.

From there, you next define the *standards of engagement*, or how they are expected to treat others when interacting or making decisions on behalf of your company on a daily basis.

Behavioral Standard for Innovation (example):

I will not dismiss someone's idea, no matter how silly or impractical I think it is.

The idea behind establishing behavioral standards is to make the value you have defined real and practical for the stakeholder. Without the behavioral expectations and standards of engagement clearly defined, a value term and broad definition is simply an idea left open to interpretation.

ASSESSMENTS: DEFINE

Are your values defined? Do your leaders behave acceptably and per those definitions?

For Step 2: Define, we start with an evaluation of your leaders' attitudes and behaviors (LAB) as exhibited through observation and formal evaluation. This assessment is centered on identifying how well your leaders understand, connect with, and apply the behavioral principles behind the company values deemed paramount to the organizations' success. This includes an assessment of the core skills or competencies that we know to be critical for the execution of work.

ASSESSMENT: LEADERSHIP ATTITUDES AND BEHAVIORS (LAB) STUDY

- **Definition:** A qualitative and quantitative diagnostic tool designed to measure the level of awareness and comprehension of the distinct leadership skills and behaviors critical to driving positive operational performance outcomes that *also* align with an organization's cultural vision.
- **Objective:** To provide insight into the skills and behavioral development opportunities among leaders and measure and validate the level of alignment to the desired company culture expressed by leaders.

An aspect of the LAB Study includes an observation of leaders in their work environment to identify how their natural and intuitive leadership behaviors align with the organization's expectations and standards. The root of our subject matter expertise includes the empirical understanding of the behaviors that perpetuate the most common and fundamental value systems, thus enabling us to accurately assess whether or not those values are being practiced. From there, we report on our findings and identify misalignment between the ideal state and the present.

What are the skills paramount to driving positive operational performance outcomes?

Do your frontline leaders demonstrate them?

In the LAB Study, we examine leaders' understanding of how to practice specific skills and behaviors within their work environment. This assessment equips us with visibility into their capacity of understanding the organization's values and whether or not they are capable of practicing the defined behaviors.

It's one thing to have a vision of how you want your leaders to behave and interact, but it's another thing to determine whether or not they have the capacity and understanding for it.

Is it reasonable or rational for you to expect someone to behave in a manner they're incapable of, or don't understand, or have not acquired the skills to demonstrate?

This measure of awareness leads to a level of cultural consciousness that is indicative of the cultural performance pillars you have established in your organization; it's the next evolution in your realization of a unified company culture.

The LAB study evaluates whether leaders' attitudes and behaviors align with the company culture's best practices. How they answer informs their likelihood to practice the company's core values.

It will also reveal how conscious they are of the importance of the behavior. Whether you've defined your values and articulated aligned behavioral expectations or not, if your leaders understand the importance of the values and behavior, it will shine through. If your leaders *don't* connect with the values and behaviors you've deemed paramount for the success of your business, you will know cultural consciousness doesn't exist.

ACTIONABLE BEHAVIORS

We help our clients attach actionable behaviors to their value systems because in our experience, of the 80 percent of organizations that have a general company value system, only 30 percent define the behavioral expectations of their values to the extent that genuine ownership and accountability surrounding these values is fostered or perpetuated. Even fewer have defined their standards for engagement.

Dictionaries provide standard definitions so we can have a common understanding. They also provide pronunciation, variant spellings, and correct grammatical usage. In a way, dictionaries also demonstrate how words behave.

Once clear and concise leadership behavior expectations and standards for engagement have been defined, it's time to connect these terms to when and where real company culture is nurtured—at the front line.

We'll do that in Pillar #3 of the culture performance management system: Connect.

CHAPTER 8

PILLAR #3

CONNECT

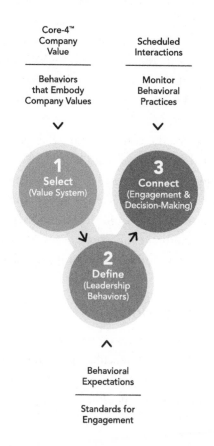

It is the dream of almost every child to learn how to ride a bike. It represents speed, freedom, and the idea of growing up. Whether they figure it out and take off on their first try, or wipe out and scrape both their elbows and a knee, it's a major milestone most will always remember.

Do you know how to ride a bike? If you do, do you remember how you learned to ride it?

First you learned what a bike was—how it functioned in a broad context (*Select*). Then you learned the rider's role to operate the bike: how they should sit, pedal, brake, balance, etc. (*Define*). After that, you decided to find somewhere to actually practice how to operate the bike, since everything up until then was conceptual or theoretical. You considered, "Where do people ride bikes? Where would I encounter scenarios that would require me to brake, pedal faster, or balance?"

You needed to make the connection to what you learned and what you wanted to practice. That's what the Connect Pillar is all about—understanding where leaders must apply these standards of practice, so you are enabled to support the learning and development process. As a senior leader, understanding when and where these cultural connections occur activates real-time observation, coaching, and feedback for the frontline leader.

CULTURAL CONNECTIONS

Defining your company values to the extent described earlier in this book is one of the most difficult steps to climb when developing and implementing your CPM system. However, overcoming the complexities of the Define Pillar will equip you with the foundational elements of what we call the Connect Pillar. This pillar focuses on *cultural connections.*

Cultural Connections: *Where and when defined leadership behaviors must be practiced during the daily execution of work.*

We have worked with senior leaders, in multiple industry verticals including food and beverage processing, automotive, and pharmaceutical, just to mention a few. In many cases, we were charged with examining where the breakdowns in leadership culture occurred for our partners. In fulfillment of this objective, one of the basic questions we would ask was:

When your frontline leaders engage with their machine operators, are they perpetuating the organization's company values?

Oftentimes, client responses included:

- "I don't know."
- "I'm not sure."
- "I don't think so."

If you don't know what these connection points are, or where and when they occur, then you can't proactively and consistently observe and evaluate whether the culture you desire is fostered. We often remind our prospective clients that "culture is still happening" with or without your expressed knowledge or visibility into the factors that either promote or detract from your desired company culture and performance outcomes.

How are your frontline leaders interacting and engaging?

What are their behaviors and day-to-day practices?

Understanding when and where interactions happen and decisions are made is the heartbeat of managing your company culture. Learning on theory without practice is unpredictable and difficult to scale or sustain. Therefore, making the "connection" between values is paramount to your culture performance management approach.

To fully connect your values, you need to observe and document your leaders' interactions at all connection points.

- They initiated a morning communication huddle.
- They did a full site walkthrough but failed to talk to any machine operator; they only focused on assets and equipment, and not the people.
- They were safety conscious and engaged employees about their understanding of our safety protocols.

As your leaders practice the behaviors, over time the employees will reciprocate. This is how companies like Chick-fil-A create a company culture that everyone can feel (experience) the moment they walk through corporate HQ's or even a storefront's doors.

ASSESSMENTS: CONNECT

For Pillar #3: Connect, the assessment includes an examination of the perceived challenges facing your frontline leaders at the point of execution, where culture happens.

In other words, this is an opportunity to solicit your leaders' perspectives regarding the factors that contribute to their ability to reach an optimal level of engagement, interaction, and decision-making. Your leaders are engaged in what we call "cultural connections" throughout the day—where critical direction is given and decisions are made. Therefore, understanding when and where these connections occur, and the factors that impact outcomes, is essential to addressing gaps in your CPM system.

We have chosen various methods to solicit cultural connection insight from frontline leaders, including the use of customized and sequenced *Culture Discovery Interviews.*

After we've finished with the discovery interviews, we move on to *Connection Mapping* to further explore where there may be breakdowns in communication that influence a leader's ability to effectively engage, interact, and make decisions for the business.

ASSESSMENT: CULTURE DISCOVERY INTERVIEWS AND CONNECTION MAPPING

- **Definition:** A qualitative diagnostic used to solicit perspectives and insights from leaders regarding the factors that contribute to their ability to reach an optimal level of engagement, interaction, and decision-making.
- **Objective:** Foster trust and transparency among leaders by encouraging open and honest reflection on the barriers they encounter when attempting to engage and interact with employees, pinpoint the factors that positively or negatively influence how leaders engage with employees and make decisions, and identify the critical cultural connections during the execution of work where interactions occur between internal stakeholders.

Do you feel confident engaging and interacting with your team? What challenges come up?

What are the factors that positively influence your team interactions? What negatively influences them?

Where do critical engagements happen between stakeholders?

During these assessments, we uncover many variables that influence how leaders drive communication and engagement during the execution of work, to the extent that we often begin to identify an organization's culture crux.

Culture Crux: *The core issues underlying a company culture—an essential point requiring problem identification and behavioral resolution.*

A culture crux is typically a foundational issue or challenge facing a leadership group that contributes to their inability to achieve their desired culture. It invokes distrust and disseminates underlying cultural issues throughout the organization, causing a significant ripple effect on all business areas, from communication to decision-making.

LOOK FOR PRACTICAL NUANCES

When you think about any human relationship, the most significant breakdowns are spurred by a lack of trust. We recommend sniffing out an organization's culture crux. When you do, don't look at the emotional responses most leaders have to perceived issues and challenges; look for more practical nuances that reveal what's going on in the business. Extrapolate data by looking for behavioral breakdowns and value misalignments.

Your leaders are the individuals who preserve and pass along the company's culture—they're demonstrating how to behave and interact with others in accordance with the organization's values, thus perpetuating "social learning" with your frontline employees as the standard for how they should behave and interact with one another as well—thanks to social learning theory.

Thinking back to riding a bike for the first time, once you have made the connection between the pedals and the bike's velocity, it's time to learn how to operate the bike and ride.

Pillar #4 of the culture performance management system, Learn, is up next.

CASE STUDY: FAIL TO SCALE

A highly recognizable global clothing retailer believes strongly in social responsibility and communication of their organization's core values. However, they struggle with implementing their cultural vision, because there is a demographic mix of employees, clients, and management styles, and they all influence individual store culture.

If you've ever worked retail, you know each store has a life all its own. If you don't have a framework and methodology around standardizing your culture, you won't be able to scale it—each retail location will have a unique microculture.

The major retailer's culture broke down at the individual store level because the organization lost sight of its core values. They didn't have a mechanism to implement or practice the behaviors associated with their values—they were defined in broad context, by the organization's founders, and were disconnected with the behaviors demonstrated at the store level.

The values themselves were okay, but how they were defined didn't relate to the frontline employees. Also, operational outcomes at the store-to-store level weren't overlaid with their cultural vision—they didn't have a cultural standard framework that could be implemented at the store level, so they couldn't scale it.

What made this organization so renowned and so powerful couldn't be replicated at the store level. Instead of one company culture, each store operated like a franchise.

This major retailer had no methodology to define, deploy, or manage their company culture, so they couldn't scale it. As a result, it reported its biggest losses in the company's half-a-century history (almost $1 billion) and filed for bankruptcy.

CHAPTER 9

PILLAR #4

LEARN

In our thirty-five years of combined experience, we've encountered organizations at various stages of the CPM system implementation, and over time we have learned that 99.9 percent of leaders struggle with reaching and *surpassing* the learning process.

Training and development in this fast-paced, digital world is tough for almost every organization—most are still utilizing classroom-style learning that isn't centered on behavioral expectations, standards for engagement, or the tactical aspects of leadership that influence how employees are motivated to perform and overcome challenges. Instead, traditional learning programs focus on technical execution resulting in employees who are "book smart" but are unable to execute in the field.

If a coach wants to improve his batter's hit percentage, is he more likely to sit this batter in front of a TV, lecture to them in a classroom, or put a bat in this batter's hand to practice the principles, starting with the fundamentals?

The ultimate objective of any investment in your leaders' development process is for them to retain new concepts and apply them in work execution. This is equally important when driving the learning process surrounding the behaviors that embody the culture you are actively implementing. It's not good enough to simply share your company values, provide clear definitions for the behavioral expectations and standards of engagement, or even identify where to practice these behaviors, because one cannot assume the leader knows how to practice them in a manner that is most effective and meaningful to the business. This is why the Learn Pillar is so critical to your CPM system implementation and sustainability.

Consider the bike-riding example shared in this Connect chapter. It isn't until you roll the bike outdoors, sit on the seat, and put on your protective gear (if you have any—when we were growing up, we sure didn't) you can begin to ride.

Your ability to apply what is shared is only possible because of real-time experience and practice. That's what the Learn Pillar is all about—someone holding the bike steady and providing you with guidance and feedback while you learn how to ride. No one is perfect, meaning everyone will fail from time to time. The Learn Pillar picks you up when you fall and puts you back on the bike. Real-time experience and practice, from a management perspective, is the only way to drive impactful and sustainable development. Learning on demand and on-the-job training is critical for *all* employees, and teaching behavioral expectations and standards for engagement should be the same.

Fortunately, since the late 1950s, researchers in the field of learning and development have acknowledged the fact that the retention rate of learners is drastically improved when applying what we call "active learning" methods as described in the Learning Pyramid image. It has been over sixty years since this first concept was introduced, yet many organizations fail to put this important concept into practice!

Training should be accessible for all learning types: visual, auditory, and kinesthetic. However, adopting more participatory learning methods will drive the greatest likelihood of retention. For example, you may consider providing your leaders with microburst learning opportunities, like podcasts, videos, or graphics, that highlight the key behaviors they should practice right before the time when they need to display these behaviors. This will help drive behavioral change over time. Using only one learning mode, such as passive methods like classroom lecture, has the lowest likelihood of retention.

Adapted from the NTL Institute of Applied
Behavioral Science Learning Pyramid

Source: "Learning Pyramid," the NTL Institute of Applied Behavioral Science

ASSESSMENTS: LEARN

It's one thing to believe you can do something, but it's another to have the competency. Someone may think they can learn how to be a medical doctor; however, their competency to perform at the necessary level is a different measurement.

Cultural Competence: *The degree to which an organization successfully and efficiently manages and consistently exhibits and drives behavior toward its ideal cultural state—an organization's ability to consistently and effectively manifest the behaviors that exemplify its company culture.*

An assessment of your organization's cultural competence should include an examination of the following:

- Through observation and leadership performance assessments, how well do your leaders engage and interact with their employees?
- Are your leaders advancing members of their teams through the necessary training mechanisms?
- Do your leaders model the organization's values?
- Is there a culture performance management system in place to help your leaders reach your desired company culture?

Cultural competence can be evaluated through a qualitative or quantitative lens. For example, what is the percentage of cultural capacity that's being met? If you're only achieving 60 percent of your cultural capacity, that's your cultural competence.

Every professional athlete's competence is measured before they're signed. Coaches and scouts look at an athlete's game knowledge, skill development, and overall mastery.

Cultural competence is no different—are employees and front-line leaders competently modeling the organization's values and behaviors? If they aren't, what skills and training do they need to get them there?

That's where our *Leadership Skills Development System Critique* assessment comes into play.

ASSESSMENT: LEADERSHIP SKILLS DEVELOPMENT SYSTEM CRITIQUE

- **Definition:** A qualitative and quantitative assessment of optimized learning and systems elements typically found in a world-class organization that supports the training and development of leaders.
- **Objective:** To identify the gaps within the current learning system that need to be filled, upgraded, or better utilized to improve its effectiveness and ensure the appropriate tools and resources are in place to support and reinforce frontline leadership team learning objectives; i.e., development resources, tools, materials, etc.

It's one thing to have an expectation of new hires and frontline employees and managers; it's another to provide the mechanism to learn those behaviors. You can interview them and train them, but how do you optimize? You have to assess where they are and then teach them how to behave:

- Is the system defined?
- Are there training materials?
- What is the decision-making criteria and mechanism for recurrent development?
- What technical and behavioral skills are needed?
- What is the system's capacity to provide training support?

This assessment establishes leaders can be properly onboarded, trained, and developed around the behaviors that define your company culture. Otherwise, you aren't setting them up for success.

TEACH A MAN TO FISH

Classroom training has evolved to try and encapsulate new theories around learning and enablement, but active learning and development methods generate autonomy and independence. It's like the old parable: *Give a man a fish, and you feed him for a day. Teach a man to fish, and you feed him for life.* On-demand training enables employees to be self-sufficient, which allows for self-evaluation and reflection. Creating a strategic learning environment that fosters real-time and practical learning is what sticks.

Strategic Learning Environment: *A specifically orchestrated systematic series of developmental activities (including engagement sessions, forum boards, knowledge testing, and practicum) designed to develop superior frontline leadership behaviors to support a focused, aligned, and accountable leader for your organization.*

How do you orchestrate the learning process around the developmental needs of your leaders? First, you have to understand where you have the greatest opportunity for a focused effort to develop their behaviors. Then you have to ensure the effort is strategic and customized to align with their needs. This means a narrow focus on the behaviors that directly align with the skills and competencies you know to be critical to driving positive outcomes for your business. Once you have installed mechanisms to foster learning among your leaders (like Read, See, Hear, Do, an empirically proven principle that captures all three learning styles: visual, auditory, and kinesthetic), you'll level up to Pillar #5 of the culture performance management system: Practice.

CHAPTER 10

PILLAR #5

PRACTICE

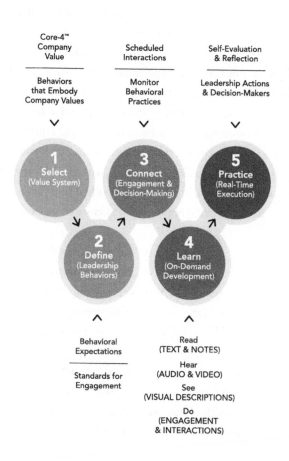

Simone Biles is tied with Larisa Latynina (a Ukrainian gymnast who competed in the 1950s and '60s) as the most decorated gymnast of all time. She has twenty-five World Artistic Gymnatics Championships and seven Olympic medals. In 2016, she made history as the first female gymnast to win four consecutive USA Gymnastics National Championships.

She got to where she is today through hard work and practice. She first learned the sport of gymnastics then practiced it.

Understanding and learning the behaviors that align with the organization's values generate genuine awareness (cultural consciousness), which enables leaders to practice what they have learned in real time, where company culture is truly impacted. However, practice is really about one's applied understanding of what, when, why, and *how* these behaviors impact how others are engaged and decisions are made. The active learning process is effective to the extent that the supervisor has a mechanism to pause and reflect, through self-evaluation, how one's actions and decisions impact specific outcomes. It's important to understand that, with any learning process that requires behavioral change, an individual must acknowledge their own developmental opportunities before change can occur.

Picture having a small wound on your arm. It's slowly bleeding and possibly infected, but you've grown so accustomed to it that you become unaware of it. You keep moving along, but meanwhile, it's getting worse, and you are beginning to impact others who are disgusted by its appearance or simply concerned.

Oftentimes, your leaders' behaviors and interactions are not conducive to fostering a positive or productive work environment; however, the individual has become so accustomed to behaving in such a manner that they don't realize its true impact.

Now, imagine a friend comes to you and says you have a wound that is bleeding and looks infected and that others are disgusted by its appearance. For motivations unknown, you ignore the wound. It doesn't matter how much your friend desires for you to change, it's only possible if *you* acknowledge the wound.

The same principle applies to a leader's behavioral change. It's only possible when a leader acknowledges their behavior and how it may be impacting others. When that happens, behavioral breakthroughs occur.

When employees experience leaders who are conscious and intentional in how they engage and interact, they are more likely to engage and reciprocate those behaviors because their behavior has become the standard that everyone follows. In realizing your desired company culture, practice is where real change begins to occur.

To promote self-awareness and behavioral consciousness, ask your leaders reflective questions such as:

- How well did you prepare to practice _____ behavior, during your last culture connection point?
- Did you understand and practice XX behavior?
- What do you believe went well when practicing XX behavior?
- What would you improve during your next culture connection when practicing XX behavior?

Most people will naturally critique themselves favorably, but these questions force them to critically examine their behaviors when interacting with others.

ASSESSMENTS: PRACTICE

Practice means improvement. This idea works for performance *and* culture. However, implementing processes that ensure acceptable behaviors are practiced without understanding leaders' capacity to do so could mean wasted resources. The leaders' cultural capacity must first be measured.

> **Cultural Capacity:** *The specific ability of an organization or resource to consistently attain a degree of excellence in demonstrating the ideal set of management and the frontline leader behaviors required to achieve 100 percent attainment of operational capacity.*

An organization's cultural capacity is its vision of the future. To understand it, a roadmap needs to be established. However, keep in mind that cultural capacity can *only* be realized if an organization's leaders have the psychological and emotional capacity to live up to the company's values (and exhibit acceptable behaviors) daily.

We use a *Leader Behavioral DILO ("day in the life")* assessment to measure this.

> ### ASSESSMENT: LEADER BEHAVIORAL DILO "DAY IN THE LIFE OF"
>
> - **Definition:** An observational, qualitative diagnostic study used to identify what, when, and where leaders impact the business through their level of engagement and interaction in the work environment and how their behaviors are perpetuated in "real time."
> - **Objective:** To examine and evaluate opportunities related to leadership engagement and decision-making, and to observe whether interactions and behaviors align with cultural performance expectations.

As a corporate executive, you have to ask yourself:

- What is the capacity of my frontline leaders to understand and practice our company values?
- How do they engage and interact with their peers and employees?
- How do these interactions influence decisions that are made throughout the day?
- How do the observed behaviors and interactions align with the organization's cultural performance expectations?
- What are the opportunities and challenges that influence those interactions and decisions?

There are core leadership skills and competencies that are fundamental to an effective management operating system. A Leader Behavioral DILO measures the perception and understanding of those competencies and validates them. It *also* measures what is or isn't essential and gaps that need to be addressed. The first step of the assessment evaluates leaders' capacity, followed by identifying the actions needed to practice and improve upon the behaviors that align with company values.

Our Leader Behavioral DILO allows us to understand the attitudes and behaviors of our clients' frontline leaders and employees from their point of view. It's not a managerial assessment—it's an evaluation of their perception and understanding of the values and behaviors to measure alignment.

We want to create profiles for our leaders so that we can leverage their skills and competencies. These profiles will help us better measure gaps, operational capacity, and limitations.

Let's say you drive a Honda. You may dream of it performing

like a Lamborghini, but at the end of the day, it's a *Honda*, so you need to understand the capacity of a Honda! What tools and resources do you need to invest in to get your Honda to perform at its full potential?

Typically, most frontline leaders exhibit a gap in the core behaviors necessary to realize their cultural potential effectively. Their capacity is rarely fully realized—many of the people placed in those leadership roles have been identified based on their technical, rather than tactical, cultural capacity. They've been identified because of their work execution and task performance, but they were never equipped to perform effectively because no one defined how their roles, or behavioral expectations, changed.

This lack of preparedness is especially true for cultural performance. It's less about performing at an optimal speed and more about measuring how well employees are engaged, trained, and developed.

What's the retention rate?

How well are promotions perpetuated?

In most organizations (mainly manufacturing and heavy and light industrial), when the existing lead operator's performance is lacking, another operator gets the lead role, but we argue this is a fundamental disconnect. If behavioral expectations are unknown, how can anyone be determined a good fit for leadership? The ability to practice the behaviors that align with the company's values is usually never vetted, primarily because they've never been effectively defined.

Cultural capacity is a company's ideal cultural state, but it can only be achieved if leadership is aligned on values and behaviors and knows how to practice them.

PRACTICE BEHAVIORAL EXPECTATIONS AND STANDARDS

Why do you think gymnastics great Simone Biles can always hit a perfect landing? Because she has critically examined it and worked hard to improve it. She practiced her landing so much that now she can *feel when it's perfect.* Landing well has become her standard.

When behavioral expectations and standards for engagement are practiced, they become intuitive and habitual. However, using the wrong form to practice your golf swing or stick the perfect landing is just as bad as not practicing at all—hence the importance of feedback. When the leader reaches a point of self-awareness and acknowledgement of their behavioral actions and implications, change is inevitable. However, to achieve an optimal state, one must measure said change to understand if it is progressive or regressive.

So, how do you measure change in behavior? You'll find out in Pillar #6 of the culture performance management system: Measure.

CHAPTER 11

PILLAR #6

MEASURE

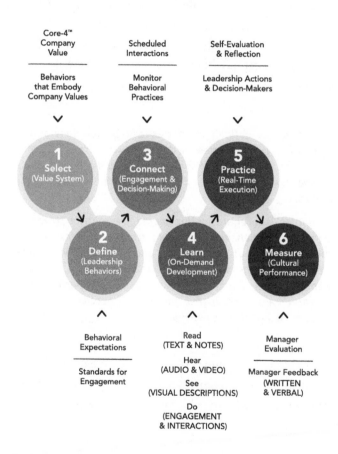

Tiger Woods, an American professional golfer, is tied for first in PGA Tour wins, ranked second in men's major championships, and holds numerous golf records. During interviews, he often reflects on when he first learned what he needed to work on to become an Olympic-caliber golfer. He admittedly watched videos of his golf swing in real time, while simultaneously receiving and applying feedback from his coaches along the way. No magic wand. Just self-reflection, feedback, discipline, practice, and *measurement*.

Pillar #6: Measure is similar in that it promotes the evaluation and validation of your leaders' ability to exhibit the expected behaviors and standards for engagement and identifies any gaps or areas for improvement. This is both written and verbal feedback. The feedback should be captured in a manner that can be validated and trended, so a "core score" or performance result can be generated.

> **Core Score:** *A defined set of metrics reported daily and/or weekly that demonstrates the degree to which frontline supervisors and managers are demonstrating and driving actions and behaviors in support of an organization's desired company culture.*
>
> *Examples: Aggregate testing scores and metrics (tracking percentage of behavior attainment, frontline leadership skills, management tools, compliance, and effective communications). The analysis of the top four core values a company wants to focus on is the organization's cultural performance score—it's a primary metric and helps proactively measure leaders' demonstrated behaviors.*

Feedback about leadership performance and capability should be shared daily, and in real time, to afford the leader the opportunity to course-correct with the objective of having a positive impact in short intervals.

Why?

To win the culture game!

ASSESSMENTS: MEASURE

There will be variance when measuring company culture—a culture centerline evaluates that variance because it represents the behavioral standards for your organization. Not all your frontline leaders will behave in 100 percent accordance with your behaviors and values 100 percent of the time—your culture centerline helps you evaluate how far away you are from your optimal state.

Culture Centerline: *Pulling from statistical process control, a culture centerline is the control point for measuring and tracking variation in cultural performance management. Deviations from the centerline indicate variability in behavior, which drives organizational company culture. Variability/deviation too far from the centerline triggers leadership that something has shifted in attitude, belief, or behavior and should be examined, understood, and addressed.*

Ultimately, a culture centerline helps optimize company culture because it will reveal whether an organization's changes move the culture needle in the right direction. Negative variance means it's regressing, and positive variance means it's moving closer to the company's ideal cultural state. Both need to be measured for a deep understanding of what works and what doesn't. For this, we use a *Culture Performance Management System Effectiveness Critique.*

**ASSESSMENT: CULTURE
PERFORMANCE MANAGEMENT SYSTEM
EFFECTIVENESS CRITIQUE**

- **Definition:** An assessment of elements we typically find in a world-class organization to support management of the leadership culture and associate processes.
- **Objective:** To determine opportunities within the current system that need to be upgraded or have better utilization.

When a company has effectively practiced the behaviors that align with their values, we need to next figure out if it worked and how well:

- Is the existing CPM system effective?
- What worked and what didn't?
- Are there upgrade possibilities within the current system?

Many organizations will get hung up thinking their optimal cultural state should always have 100 percent employee engagement, but that's an unrealistic expectation, *especially* if using the CPM system has given them their first visibility into their culture.

Let's say your culture centerline is 56 percent—is it reasonable to expect 100 percent *all* of the time? Wouldn't it be better to see a positive variance and upward trajectory, so you can measure and understand the behavioral practices driving cultural performance improvement?

A culture centerline helps you align your entire organization under *one* cultural vision that you believe will help you fulfill your mission, vision, and purpose. By aligning everyone accordingly, you will have the greatest potential of success without detraction—

one centerline establishes a focal point, so everyone strives for the same goal. It ensures everyone is behaving, interacting, and engaging similarly. A culture centerline tells your leaders, "This is required for us to be successful as an organization."

Think about wheel alignment—when all four wheels of a car are aligned, its performance is optimized. When the wheels aren't aligned, the car's entire performance is compromised. That doesn't mean it stops running, but optimization is impossible. The car also suffers from more wear and tear, meaning its mechanical integrity has been compromised. The car also suffers from decreased miles per gallon, hence you need more fuel (energy) to drive this proverbial car 100 miles than the fuel required to drive the car 100 miles when the tires are properly aligned. As a leader in your business, are you having to expend extra energy and time because your culture is not aligned?

Wheel alignment is critical for optimal vehicle performance, just like cultural alignment is essential for optimal business performance. Alignment can only be attained if everyone is focused on the same goals and has a standard for comparison. A culture centerline provides that.

MEASURE YOUR SUCCESS

Measurement is a part of every professional athlete's regime, not only Tiger Woods'.

Have you ever watched a major sporting event that involved players and coaches? Let's consider the game of professional football in the US and specifically the position of quarterback. Throughout the game, what happens after nearly every play-drive? After the quarterback completes the play with the passing of the ball—

regardless if the outcome is positive or negative when the drive is over—he heads to the sideline and two things happen:

1. He reviews the prior play to identify what he could have done better or he interprets what worked well so he can repeat it (self-reflection),
2. He has a conversation with the coach to receive feedback to understand how to run the most optimal play in the future and what needs to happen for the next play (manager feedback).

The result of the play generates metrics, such as "pass completion rate," the team uses to judge the effectiveness of the quarterback. It's not about the score that was generated at the end of the play, or if the game was won or lost. To impact the game while it is in play, the coaches focus on the players' performances in real time. Feedback regarding the specific behaviors that reflect their performance is the focal point. The measurement of success is predicated on the feedback given and received and how application of this feedback drives improvement in short interval. The long-term effect will be the sustainable advancement of your cultural performance.

Now, what happens when feedback is given, and course-correction is underway?

What happens with the insights one may obtain with performance measurement?

It's time to move to Pillar #7 of the culture performance management system: Refine.

CHAPTER 12

PILLAR #7

REFINE

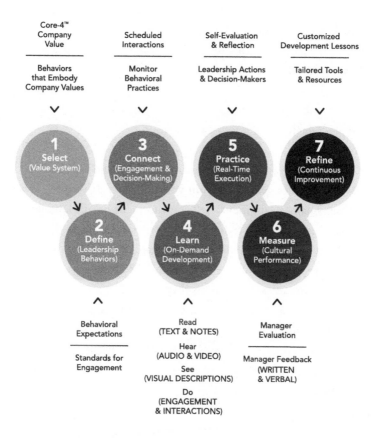

MTV Cribs is a documentary TV series that takes viewers on a tour of celebrities' private homes. It initially aired in September of 2000 and is still produced (and distributed via Snapchat) today. On the show, the stars themselves give the tour and typically showcase their homes' most impressive features, like indoor swimming pools, garages filled with luxury sports cars, and massive home theaters.

These homes are spectacular because they've been refined to the celebrity homeowner's specific taste—that is what makes the show interesting to watch.

Refine means to fine-tune and hone. An *MTV Cribs* celebrity who loves to collect rare cars, for example, will likely have a home with a big garage to store them. Their home has been fine-tuned to accommodate their hobby.

The last pillar of the culture performance management process is Refine, which requires two considerations:

1. **How will your leaders continue to leverage the feedback and metrics generated from your CPM to drive their own personal development?** Self-improvement means leveraging the resources and technology leaders have at their disposal. What are the mechanisms your organization has in place to ensure leaders drive their development? How do you ensure they have access to the tools they need?
2. **How do you focus on cultural progression, rather than a static, one-time score?** Continuous improvement means closely evaluating cultural performance alongside other business metrics. Other metrics are influenced by how leaders engage and interact, too.

> **Core Workout:** *The management process of actively compar-ing self-evaluation of real-time behaviors to the cultural ideal of a manager's evaluation of the same behaviors, and then engaging in active discussion and development to move these behaviors closer to the ideal.*

An investment in your company culture shouldn't be treated as a short-term business initiative, or a one-time implementation and execution event. A focus on refinement means the perpetual identification of opportunities for continuous improvement of the complete CPM system (all seven pillars) and the tools and processes that support it. It means executive management is dili-gent in the measurement and practice of the leadership behaviors and standards for engagement that reflect the optimal company culture.

ASSESSMENTS: REFINE

Finally, we want to determine how we can best help our clients *refine* their company culture. For this, we need a *Communication Effectiveness Study*.

> ### ASSESSMENT: COMMUNICATION
> ### EFFECTIVENESS STUDY
>
> - **Definition:** Series of criteria, based on empirical observa-tions, that use qualitative and quantitative data collection methods to check behavioral alignment and how employ-ees are treated.
> - **Objective:** To examine how leaders communicate with employees and each other and the tools used to facilitate communication.

Your CPM measurements, and the mechanisms you implement to refine them, become directionally foundational for your company. A Communication Effectiveness Study can serve as a culture compass to help executive management determine if their company culture is headed in the right direction.

- Do they have the mechanisms in place to foster value-added exchanges throughout the day?
- Does their communication motivate and mobilize?
- Does it clarify expectations?

If you're engaged in an exchange with your peers, and the objective is to clarify everyone's project execution roles and responsibilities, an agenda needs to be set, meeting notes need to be documented, and next steps need to be established. Set clear expectations, deadlines, and best practices, in order to yield the desired result: alignment.

Culture Compass: *The method and tool that allows managers to frequently ensure their cultural interactions and behaviors are in sync with the cultural requirements.*

Change to your company culture is less about the numbers and more about incremental improvements in the right direction. If I know my cultural baseline and all the steps I need to take to improve my centerline, all I need is a cultural compass to point me how to get there. Cultural performance management provides me with it—it's an outcome of having a CPM system in place.

UNDERSTAND THE OPPORTUNITIES

Refinement is best executed by first understanding opportunities facing each leader's ability to practice the behaviors that embody the company's value system, then by building individualized or team-centric performance development plans that include the use and application of tools and resources that promote continuous learning, evaluation, and feedback. We recommend a balance of active and passive learning and development methods. For example, role-playing in a classroom setting, coupled with real-time observation and feedback from peers in the practice of those same scenarios.

Furthermore, *Refine* also translates to the accompanying CPM system pillars. The system ensures behavioral standards and expectations are clear and don't waiver; however, that doesn't mean they shouldn't be reevaluated for the purpose of optimization. Don't lose sight of how the business is evolving and how your CPM system supports this growth. You may find extended definitions or clarity surrounding your value system, behavioral standards, and connection points, or your learning and measurement process may warrant some fine-tuning. Be sure to address the language you use to clarify your performance expectations. For example, ask yourself, as new roles and job descriptions are developed, if they accurately reflect or align with the company culture performance framework you have developed.

We have found that most organizations understand company culture is pivotal to their future success, and oftentimes this responsibility has been placed in the hands of human resource (HR) management professionals. The challenge with that direction, however, is that HR typically isn't operationally focused and doesn't fully understand the training and developmental needs of frontline leaders and employees. There is a disconnect that occurs because these internal divisions are often siloed.

Where does your company culture stack up in the systems used to measure, manage, and scale? What does your organization need to work on?

HEALTHY COMPANY CULTURE

Healthy company culture will be sculpted by the values, behaviors, and interactions between stakeholders, from senior leaders to the front line and back again. Assess the company culture so you can fix it, because when you fix the company culture, the employee experience will fix itself.

Culture performance management is an ongoing journey and needs steering at the required points of inflection. It also requires continuous reinforcements and role modeling from the leadership team. Ensure that you keep frontline leaders and employees engaged by showing them the impact of the values, behaviors, and interactions on performance.

A homeowner can't make a repair or perform maintenance on their home without first assessing the problem that needs to be fixed. The celebrities who make appearances on *MTV Cribs* have to assess their house issues and then make the right repairs before they can refine them. It's a simple, step-by-step process.

Now that you know the steps in our culture performance management system and how to assess where a company's culture stacks up in relation to it, it's time to move to the next phases of the journey: operationalization, optimization, and continuous improvement.

CASE STUDY: IS YOUR CULTURE A NOVELTY?

We met with the CEO of a novelty gift shop chain, popular in the northeast US. As we sat in a conference room in their Secaucus, New Jersey, headquarters he told us he spent $300,000 in team-building events for his staff annually and didn't understand why his turnover rate was so high. He needed our help to figure it out.

So, we did some research. We attended a holiday party at one of their plants, to see one of the company's team-building events in action, and watched as employees rolled their eyes at the perceived frill.

We also directly surveyed employees to compare what they found important, versus what executive management found important, regarding workplace engagement. The results told us that employees preferred in-depth onboarding and training and development to parties and off-sites.

Finally, we took a look at the attrition data and discovered the highest turnover rates occurred within the first two weeks of employment. The company had a major issue sourcing, screening, and onboarding new employees, so we recommended they move their team-building and employee events budget to recruiting, onboarding, and training and development.

These executive leaders knew how to run a highly successful novelty shop, but they treated their company culture like a novelty and it backfired.

Company culture is real and isn't a novelty. If you treat it as such, your employees will see right through it.

PART 3

OPERATIONALIZATION, OPTIMIZATION, AND CONTINUOUS CULTURAL IMPROVEMENT

CHAPTER 13

OPERATIONALIZE YOUR CULTURE

The first "online" shopping experience happened in 1984, before the invention of the internet. Michael Aldrich, an English inventor, wanted to help the elderly, disabled, and impaired with their grocery orders, so he developed Videotex, a network of closed computer terminals that called shoppers orders into supermarkets. (The tech allowed shoppers to type their orders onto their TV screens.) The groceries then appeared at the shoppers' front doors.

In 1994, online shopping appeared again, this time on the internet. Daniel M. Kohn invented NetMarket, a "shopping mall in cyberspace,"[7] where the first internet purchase was made: a Sting CD for £10. Later that year in July, Amazon.com launched.

Today, Amazon is a household name, and that likely isn't going to change any time soon. According to Pew Research, 80 percent of Americans are shopping online.[8] Every major retailer has an e-commerce website. Those that do not are behind, because these days, shoppers expect to find everything they need online.

---

7   https://www.nytimes.com/1994/08/12/business/attention-shoppers-internet-is-open.html

8   https://www.pewresearch.org/internet/2016/12/19/online-shopping-and-e-commerce/

MILLION-DOLLAR QUESTION

The invention of the internet irrevocably changed retail, just like mobile irrevocably changed e-commerce. The most successful online retailers have a website *and* a mobile app that is both user-friendly and compatible with all operating systems. They have fully operationalized the shopping experience for *all* users.

The million-dollar question isn't "How do I make my culture perfect?" it's "How do I develop the *executive management team* to embody the standards of behavior that align with the organization's values, and how do I develop and retrain them?"

Or, more simply put: "How do I operationalize my company culture?"

NOW A WORD FROM OUR SPONSOR

For most organizations, implementing and maintaining a CPM system will be tough. Retraining is undoubtedly involved, so the methodology and the approach used to retool executive management must be considered. How will they be able to demonstrate the behaviors and standards that equate to the company's values?

We understand implementing and maintaining the CPM system without a tool isn't easy, and we don't want to advertise our technology. However, the only way to show you the type of tool you need, to do the work you have to do for your culture, is to talk about ours, because it's the only one available. There are plenty of consultants with methodologies and frameworks in the "fix your culture" space, but this is the first (and only) software.

Can you develop one *without* our tool (or any tool in general, for that matter)? Yes, but it would be difficult, like driving a car without an engine. You could put it in neutral and push it to your destination, but it's going to take you a while to get there and you might injure yourself and pull something.

It's easier *and* more efficient to drive a car with an engine—it's also easier to develop your CPM process with the proper tool, a software platform we developed to support our CPM system: CultureWorx.

CultureWorx helps companies overcome the challenge of successfully implementing, improving, and sustaining a company culture that optimizes the employee experience and business performance. It is backed by behavioral science and social learning theory, getting to the root of what makes a company culture great—language, behaviors, and interactions between people in an organization.

The platform measures how well your leaders engage and interact with team members, which influences how decisions are made and performance objectives are achieved. You can:

- Review your culture performance score where culture happens—on the front line
- Evaluate manager and supervisor collaboration and feedback
- Monitor on-demand learning with customized educational resources and developmental tracks

The platform *also* enables leaders to establish ownership and accountability by:

- Facilitating daily feedback between managers and supervisors on their ability to practice leadership behaviors
- Promoting real-time microburst learning with automated distribution of audio, video, and text learning resources

Culture performance management is reinforced through the empirically supported concept that self-driven, autonomous use, and proactive visibility of processes, systems, and proper leadership behaviors drives optimal performance outcomes. These ideologies are the foundation of CultureWorx.

WHY CULTUREWORX?

CultureWorx facilitates integrity between your company's values and correlating leadership behaviors to improve your company's culture performance and improve business outcomes. It also serves as a competitive advantage for talent recruitment and retention, leadership development, and sales and business outcomes. The platform systemizes and utilizes business culture performance management.

The platform ensures standardized and scalable onboarding and training processes are implemented and promotes the learning and development of those systems and accompanying behaviors. CultureWorx helps:

1. Manage and measure the company's culture performance.
2. Scale company culture across all teams and locations.
3. Prove the company's culture to the marketplace.
4. Develop the management team with daily in-app practices.
5. Cultivate the company's culture in real time, using its individualized values.

It defines, documents, and establishes organizational leadership behaviors—CultureWorx provides standardized leadership practices and performance expectations.

1. MANAGE AND MEASURE THE COMPANY'S CULTURE PERFORMANCE.

Business leaders and HR professionals increasingly deem company culture a primary objective, yet don't have a standardized method or KPI to cultivate, measure, and enhance it. CultureWorx is the first business culture performance software for defining, implementing, measuring, and improving company culture.

The CultureWorx technology is based on empirical research, social learning theory, and years of implementation and results. It facilitates integrity between your company's values and correlating leadership behaviors, delivering an objective business culture score you can count on.

2. SCALE COMPANY CULTURE ACROSS ALL TEAMS AND LOCATIONS.

The team behind CultureWorx knows the challenges of scaling your best people, your core values, and your unique company culture across a growing organization. Whether you're adding physical locations or growing your team virtually, CultureWorx can help you define, scale, and sustain your company's culture vision, practices, and performance results.

Using our intuitive and methodical software, we help you develop and enforce a common language around your values. This will ensure everyone knows exactly what they mean and how to embody them through leadership behaviors and actions. One centralized application for one scalable company culture.

3. PROVE THE COMPANY'S CULTURE TO THE MARKETPLACE.

Workplace culture is big business. It's a competitive advantage for talent recruiting and retention, and it's influencing the way consumers, suppliers, and partners choose who to do business with. With so much riding on business culture today, CultureWorx gives you an objective way to measure it, rather than relying on opinions or moods.

Through common definitions of your values, qualified evaluations from informed employees, and an objective scoring method, CultureWorx factors out biases to produce a data-driven business culture score that you can use to prove your company culture to the marketplace.

4. DEVELOP THE MANAGEMENT TEAM WITH DAILY IN-APP PRACTICES.

A thriving business culture is not the result of static surveys, fluctuating opinions, or reactive management training—it's the consistent practice and reinforcement of proven leadership behaviors that make your company culture work.

CultureWorx packages this process for your management teams, leveraging Albert Bandura's four principles of social learning— attention, retention, reproduction, and motivation—to drive behavioral change. Daily notifications prompt your team to carry out positive leadership actions reinforced by objective, real-time scoring from others.

We use this social learning theoretical framework to underpin the cultural performance management methodology because it supports the notion that an organization's leaders are the catalyst to mobilizing an entire workforce around its desired culture. Simply put, the CPM system promotes a leader's ability to *focus* on behaviors that embody the desire culture (attention); *learn* through repetition and memory via the recollection of actions, feedback, and practice (retention); *replicate* learned behaviors (reproduction); and *connect* these actions to positive or negative consequences via tracking, feedback, reflection, etc. (motivation).

5. CULTIVATE THE COMPANY'S CULTURE IN REAL TIME, USING ITS INDIVIDUALIZED VALUES.

No two companies are exactly alike, and that's the way we like it. CultureWorx is designed to implement, improve, and scale the company culture that makes your business unique and successful. Through our software (once again, backed by empirically supported data) you will choose the company values you want to focus on each quarter, which will be mapped to proven, correlating leadership behaviors.

To improve how employees are engaged, your management teams will be prompted to proactively learn and demonstrate these behaviors, through microburst learning and real-time feedback. This is how your desired culture is cultivated daily to improve business performance.

IMPROVE LEADERSHIP BEHAVIORS

The inventions of mobile and internet technologies forced the retail industry to change. Shoppers wanted the ability to shop online and through their mobile devices, so e-commerce and mobile shopping were born. Tools and methods used to implement, measure, and maintain company culture need to adjust to the changing marketplace, too. Most workplace culture tools are reactive, static, and bottom-up and fail to facilitate an authentic environment. They are ineffective.

Our software is the first business culture performance management tool that uses empirical research and certified effective learning methods to get to the root of your organization's core values and your team's leadership behaviors. It measures, manages, and improves the actions that impact the employee experience, leadership decision-making, and business results.

CultureWorx works to improve the leadership behaviors that impact your business performance. It identifies which behaviors need to be improved, while providing developmental resources that facilitate increased engagement, reduced turnover, and improved operational performance. Whether it is trust, integrity, inclusiveness, or any other company value, CultureWorx enables your leaders to practice and improve the behaviors that you know contribute to your success.

We believe that you can't fake company culture. Having integrity behind it can create engagement and empowerment for a better employee experience and lead to improved business outcomes. CultureWorx allows you to fully harness the power of a CPM system, so you can operationalize your company culture and get control of it.

After the CPM system has been operationalized, it's time to optimize.

CHAPTER 14

OPTIMIZE YOUR CULTURE

Smallpox is an infectious disease that kills 30 percent of everyone who contracts it. The remaining 70 percent are left with severe scarring on their skin or blindness. Fortunately, in 1980 the World Health Organization (WHO) confirmed the disease has been officially eradicated.

Before it was eradicated, however, smallpox did some damage and is considered one of the deadliest diseases to infect humans.[9] It's hard to pinpoint its exact origin, but some believe it dates all the way back to the third century BCE. Physical evidence of scarring, very similar to the scarring left by smallpox, was found on Egyptian mummies.[10] Regardless, in the last one hundred years *alone*, it has killed approximately 500 million people.[11]

A disease *that is infectious* is difficult to get rid of, so how did the planet do it?

---

9   "Smallpox Vaccines," World Health Organization, May 31, 2016, https://www.who.int/news-room/feature-stories/detail/smallpox-vaccines.

10 "History of Smallpox," CDC.gov, accessed July 7, 2021, https://www.cdc.gov/smallpox/history/history.html.

11 D.A. Henderson, *Smallpox: The Death of a Disease* (Buffalo, NY: Prometheus Books, 2009), 12.

In 1776, English doctor Edward Jenner started to develop a vaccine for smallpox, and by 1801, published his findings. Less than two centuries later, the last worldwide case of smallpox occurred in the UK, after an outbreak in 1978. It is the only infectious disease ever to be eradicated by man.[12]

GETTING CULTURAL BUY-IN

Vaccinations have been a hot topic for decades.

For some of you, the question of whether or not you or your children have been vaccinated has been raised countless times. We aren't commenting on whether or not you should be vaccinated (we're ideologically neutral, remember?), we simply want you to consider vaccination ideology in the context of company culture. Are your employees genuinely bought-in and engaged with your cultural values and practices? Have they taken your "culture vaccine"?

Your employees' answer to this question is a harbinger of your employee turnover rates and overall company performance. You may find that your employees' answers will be split between those who are, those who are unsure, and those who have not bought in to your company culture, yet show up to work every day.

This correlates to behavior seen in response to the COVID-19 vaccination.

On January 7, 2021, Patrick Cawley, Chief Executive Officer of the Medical University of South Carolina Health, suggested the

---

12 "History of Smallpox."

hospital's initial vaccine response rates tracked with studies that show people split roughly into three categories:

1. Those who receive the vaccine immediately
2. Those who apply a wait-and-see approach
3. Those who decline the vaccine

In response to over twenty-four separate studies regarding the general public's response to the COVID-19 vaccine, Cawley stated:

> A third [of the population] take the vaccine right away. They will schedule it almost as soon as they can get it. And then a third [of the population] will not schedule right away. They say they want it, but they do not want to take it right away. They are scheduling [the vaccination] at the end of our scheduling [cycle]. And then you [have] about a third [of the population] who are not going to take it right now. They're [subsequently] saying absolutely no.[13]

Does this make you uncomfortable or uneasy? It should, because, ironically, a similar trend is prevalent among leaders and employees within the workplace when it comes to buy-in and adoption of your company culture. An example of data stemming from a wide variety of employee engagement/experience survey studies revealed approximately:

- 33 percent of US employees report feeling engaged by their leaders
- 33 percent moderately engaged

---

13   Zak Koeske and Sammy Fretwell, "More SC Health Care Workers Refused or Deferred COVID-19 Vaccine than Expected," TheState.com, January 10, 2021, https://www.thestate.com/news/coronavirus/article248368225.html.

- 33 percent completely disengaged.[14]

The level of perceived disengagement from the leaders is a direct reflection of their understanding, buy-in, alignment, or ownership of their company's cultural vision and practices. This breakdown prevents culture optimization from happening.

You may question, *Why do we see similarities in these two trends that otherwise seem unrelated?* The answer is simple: poor communication, and hence, poor understanding. Poor communication has contributed to the general population's hesitancy to receive the COVID-19 vaccine. It is also one of the reasons why, or why not, your leaders and employees understand and respond to your company culture.

Culture optimization means using the insights gleaned from your CPM to influence recruiting and training programs. It leverages the positive aspects of your business and mitigates the negative, so you can attract customers, vendors, and top talent.

DO YOU HAVE A HERD COMPANY CULTURE?

When leaders attempt to communicate their desired company culture, typically through sharing their vision for how specific values and behaviors (when practiced) will lead to effective engagement and subsequently drive positive business outcomes, most fail to consider the level of understanding, adoption, or buy-in required to perpetuate and sustain this culture. This is the act of achieving a *herd culture*.

---

14 Jim Hartner, "Historic Drop in Employee Engagement Follows Record Rise," Gallup.com, July 2, 2020, https://www.gallup.com/workplace/313313/historic-drop-employee-engagement-follows-record-rise.aspx.

Sound familiar? Consider this concept in relation to vaccinations. According to Dr. Anthony Fauci, Director of the National Institute of Allergy and Infectious Diseases, the objective of promoting vaccinations is to achieve *herd immunity*, or a sustained resistance to the spread of the infectious disease within the population. Dr. Fauci explained to reach herd immunity, 75 to 85 percent of the general population needs to get vaccinated.[15]

Imagine achieving a herd *culture* where 75 to 85 percent of your leaders fully understand and demonstrate the behaviors and interactions required by your company values. Your company culture is then perpetuated through the organization, with every employee. What would this mean for your business outcomes? The unfortunate reality is this herd-immunity level of cultural adoption, as exhibited by the level of engagement reported from leaders by employees, is over twice the current level of engagement reported nationally.

When attempting to achieve a herd culture (group ownership and adoption of your company culture), let us consider what the experts have done to reach a point of herd *immunity*. Begin with addressing what influences the populations' hesitancy to receive the vaccination in the first place.

COMMUNICATION AND EDUCATION

Ownership and adoption of your company culture (cultural optimization) begins with your leaders. The leadership team is 100 percent responsible for educating and demonstrating your company culture. Failure to achieve the level of buy-in to your company culture vision and associated practices often relates to

---

15 Dr. Anthony Fauci, "Live with Infectious Disease Expert, Dr. Fauci," Facebook.com, video published November 30, 2020, https://www.facebook.com/4/videos/10112595016437891.

bottlenecks in your approach to communicating this vision and educating your employees. This prevents your ability to ensure they adopt a clear and aligned understanding of how your company values must be demonstrated through specific behaviors and interactions. Furthermore, if the leaders cannot define the behaviors required that your company culture comprises, then they will never be able to communicate and educate employees on your company culture. Ignorance breeds ignorance.

When sharing your cultural vision and the expectations surrounding how individuals should engage with one another, consider how an employee is supposed to adhere to your company values when they are not "educated" on the behaviors that produce these values. The definition and meaning of the company values are often a mystery to employees due to a lack of clarity and ineffective articulation of how to practice the behaviors that exemplify these values. The behaviors managers demonstrate or exhibit as values serve as the foundation by which frontline employees will begin to frame how they should behave and interact with one another, hence the importance of promoting education regarding how to effectively practice these behaviors daily.

When companies espouse their values and display them to the world for everyone to see, they are telling all stakeholders, "This is who we are, this is how we operate, and this is what you should expect and experience when working with us." They are being prescriptive. Therefore, a company must continue to be prescriptive in defining what behaviors are expected, when, where, and how. And your leaders must also be prescriptive with the employees on what behaviors they should expect to see from their leaders that demonstrate your company values. You must pull this prescriptive thread all the way through the organization.

OPTIMIZE THROUGH OWNERSHIP

Optimizing your culture is all about practicing acceptable behaviors and fostering understanding. It's the transformation from conceptual understanding to genuine ownership. Once you've accomplished that, it's time to leverage those engagements to continue to drive positive performance outcomes.

When you drive a new car, it takes time to get used to the brakes and comfortable with the steering. As you become more familiar with the operation of your car, you can anticipate how it's going to perform on specific roads and preemptively accelerate or decelerate to maximize the effectiveness of the machine. It's a level of awareness and connection with your car that informs how you adapt as its operator.

Taking this a step further, now that you've implemented the CPM system, how do you leverage what you've learned through your increased employee engagement?

Ask yourself:

1. How are the changes in leadership engagement, interactions, and decision-making impacting employee productivity and business results?
2. How do you use that knowledge to progress your culture and your operation?

A focal point should be on increased leadership performance visibility—you can see how your leaders are actively exhibiting the behaviors that align with your company values, whether it's informing and influencing their decision-making, and their overall level of engagement.

This notion aligns with the operational concept of *plan, actual, variance, action (PAVA)*, a framework we use to explain how an organization performs against an objective it has and the action it should take. If the variance is negative, how do we mitigate? If positive, how do we exploit it?

Do leaders need more training and development?

Do you have the *right* leaders?

PAVA is the action you take after a full-body scan—what would you do with total company culture visibility?

Once your plan for your culture has been implemented, actual real-time results can be measured to evaluate a potential variance to your culture plan. If a variance has been identified (good or bad), you want to explore it and take action to resolve or leverage it accordingly. That's what optimization is all about!

If you have a variance in your culture (leader performance expectation), it begs the following questions:

1. Do you understand why?
2. Are you taking action to address it?

Once you've operationalized your culture, you need to optimize it so you can get the most out of it. It's like anything that requires maintenance. You can't buy a car and then ignore it. You have to change the oil, rotate the tires, and refill the windshield wiper fluid. You have to clean it, vacuum it, and fix it whenever it breaks down. True ownership of that car means maintaining it; otherwise it could stall out on the freeway or its engine would seize.

True ownership of *anything* requires the ability to make decisions that will sustain it as an investment. Taking ownership of company culture means the same thing—it should be nurtured and treated as an investment.

Why would executives care about culture at all if it didn't equate to an increased bottom line?

Optimizing your culture means interpreting the results of your CPM system (Pillar #6: Measure), examining how your operational and leadership culture has been impacted, and understanding where there may be opportunities to improve (Pillar #7: Refine) elements of your CPM model. For example, you may explore how the behavioral expectations and standards for engagement need to be fine-tuned in order to achieve a maximum return.

FRONTLINE LEADERS MAKE CULTURE OPTIMIZATION HAPPEN

When fine-tuning behavioral expectations and standards, frontline leaders should be center stage, because they drive company culture. The majority of employees are engaged and influenced by their frontline leaders. As a whole, they are an organization's culture control point.

> **Culture Control Point:** *Frontline leaders demonstrate value-based behaviors in action. This is the group of people to be developed and managed in order to effectively demonstrate and execute the company culture you desire. They can have the greatest positive cultural impact on your employees.*

The culture control point reflects how the frontline leaders engage and interact with employees—they should be modeling the company's culture.

When you evaluate your employees' perception of culture, it's contingent upon their perception of your *frontline* leaders' engagement, interactions, and decision-making. Frontline leaders are the culture control point of your organization—they know how to effectively execute culture and have the power to demonstrate the positive impact it has on your company.

What is the control point of your car? Is it the steering wheel *or* the person steering?

The person steering is the control point, because without them the car is inoperable.

Think about race car drivers. It doesn't matter how suited and booted the car is, without Dale Earnhardt it doesn't make it across the finish line. All the optimizations in the world are irrelevant.

Frontline leaders, as a whole, are the organization's culture control point because they make culture happen. They have the most significant impact on your employees' experience of your culture.

Whereas a collective group of frontline leaders make up a culture control point, the individual frontline leaders themselves are the culture cogs. The more cogs that are misaligned with the culture control point, the more likely the company's culture performance is going to shift in a negative direction.

Culture Cog: *The individual within an organization represents the primary driver of an outcome. In the case of CPM, they are frontline supervisors who drive appropriate behaviors, down to team members in support of desired company culture and operational efficiency. These individuals keep the wheels of an organization turning and in alignment.*

Culture cogs are individuals, which is why performance assessment and self-reflection is critical to our CPM system. Measuring and assessing culture broadly is problematic, because it won't identify individual cogs and whether they're having a positive or negative impact on company culture.

Culture cogs are important to CPM because they're similar to links in a chain—if one link is broken, the integrity of the chain is lost. When trying to optimize culture, it's critical to never lose sight of culture cogs because one negatively impacting cog can quickly turn into two or three.

Many organizations struggle with optimizing culture because they have at least one leader who doesn't care to embody its defined values and behaviors. Soon, how they engage and make decisions starts to shift, and over time, this new behavior becomes habitual. Then the cadence changes, and employees no longer witness consistent behavior. Eventually, the culture falls apart because it's only as strong as its weakest link.

WHAT'S THE FREQUENCY?

When we establish cultural connections between frontline leaders and employees, there is a frequency in which they occur. Part of establishing credibility, anticipation, and expectation around cultural connections is to ensure they are routinely scheduled. Cultural cadence is the flow of those connections and should align with scheduling communication channels, so employees can practice those behaviors consistently. From there, they will be able to anticipate, expect, recognize, and appreciate them.

Cultural Cadence: *The rhythmic pattern of a company's culture—a pattern that allows teams to know what they are doing and when it will occur. The purpose of a cadence is to establish a reliable and dependable cultural capability that demonstrates a predictable capacity.*

There is also a cadence to individual cultural connection points. There's a unique rhythm to daily startup huddles, weekly meetings, and site walk-throughs. Cultural cadence moves values and behaviors from theory to practice, because it incorporates them into the frontline leaders' daily routines. They become part of how the business lives and operates.

Cultural cadence plays into how you review and assess performance, too. There's a reason the CPM system recommends leaders self-assess a specific number of connections—it establishes the values and behaviors at those connection points as habit and thus behavior can be ingrained subconsciously over time.

If you decide to teach your child the ABCs and teach them for fifteen minutes today, do you think it's a good idea to wait five days before you sit down to teach them again? That method won't perpetuate learning or behavioral change because there's no cadence to it—it's random and chaotic, so recollection is jeopardized and habit isn't formed.

Our CPM system creates repetitions through mechanisms that best align with the learner. It's habit-forming and creates subconscious behavioral change.

Cultural cadence doesn't mean leadership behavior is robotic; it simply means consistent behavioral expectations have been defined and employees can rely on them. If employees see their frontline leaders are always early to meetings, they will come to expect it and begin to embody the behavior themselves. Their thinking becomes, *I'm going to anticipate a certain standard of behavior from my leader, and if I don't behave similarly, they're going to check me on it.* Any behavior that is repeated over time becomes the expectation.

Repeated, consistent behavior also promotes equity. *In*equity presents itself when someone believes they have been treated differently when compared to someone else. When every leader behaves and interacts with their employees the same way, no matter who they are, what they look like, or where they came from, employees will understand that is the standard. Cultural cadence ensures consistency. Consistent cultural leadership behavior ensures equity.

ENGAGING EMPLOYEES TO MEASURE SUCCESS

Many organizations use employee experience surveys to measure company culture. We suggest they be amended to reflect the CPM system.

For example, the language in the survey should reflect the behavioral expectations and standards of engagement selected and defined by the company. Leadership behaviors and interactions should align with survey questions, so the survey can be an ex post facto measurement of cultural engagement. They answer the question, *Are our efforts paying off?*

Optimization occurs when an organization makes the best or most effective use of its resources. In this case, we are referring to its leadership resources, which in turn optimize its human capital resources in general. Better engagement, interaction, and decision-making equate to increased productivity.

Engagement is key to employee retention—they want to feel like they have a purpose and that they belong. They want clarity on their role and performance expectations and the tools and resources needed to be successful.

Cultural engagement is critical for optimizing individual performance. If you don't engage with your vehicle while driving it, for instance, the car will fail you. It doesn't matter how fancy it is.

Implementing a CPM system enables organizations to mobilize their leaders to practice the values they deem essential to their operational success. The CultureWorx platform serves as a mechanism for employee engagement and optimization.

> **Cultural Engagement:** *A single-number metric used to measure how engaged the individuals within an organization are in its desired company culture. Typically, a post-metric.*

If you don't engage your employees over time, their skills will become irrelevant. They require maintenance, care, and investment, like any other business asset. Engaging with your employees ensures you will get the most out of them. You've selected values and defined behaviors you believe will drive positive outcomes for your business, but if your employees aren't engaged, what is the point?

Everything requires maintenance, even your frontline leaders' and employees' engagement with your company culture. You can't simply assess your cultural problem spots, implement the CPM system, and walk away—to optimize your company culture, you have to proactively maintain it.

You also have to get cultural buy-in from your frontline leaders and employees. Cultural buy-in leads to culture optimization, which all leads to a herd culture. (A herd culture means a large percentage of your population buys into your culture vaccine.)

In order for smallpox to be eradicated, herd immunity was needed, which meant a large percentage of the population had to be vaccinated.

Culture optimization is no different. Our CPM system could be implemented five times, but without the buy-in of frontline leaders and employees, optimization cannot happen.

Get your team on board with cultural performance management, and optimization of your company culture becomes easier.

CHAPTER 15

CONTINUOUS CULTURAL IMPROVEMENT

Arnold Schwarzenegger has had a very robust career. He first rose to fame as an Olympian and then as a professional body-builder from the 1960s through the early 1980s. He won the Mr. Olympia competition seven times and is still a prominent figure in the sport.

In the 1970s, he began the transition to Hollywood, where he also had a lot of success. He is probably most well-known for the title role in James Cameron's *Terminator* series, but in 1976, he won the Golden Globe New Star of the Year award for his role in *Stay Hungry* with Jeff Bridges. He had multiple box office successes, too: *Commando, Raw Deal, The Running Man, Predator,* and *Red Heat.* In 2003, *Terminator 3: Rise of the Machines* grossed $150 million domestically.[16]

Schwarzenegger didn't stop there. He dabbled in politics from 1990–1993, when President George H.W Bush appointed him

---

16   "Terminator 3: Rise of the Machines," boxofficemojo.com, accessed July 8, 2021, https://www.boxofficemojo.com/release/rl3413476865/.

as chairman of the President's Council on Physical Fitness and Sports[17] and ran to replace the governor of California, Gray Davis, when he was recalled in 2003. Schwarzenegger won as a write-in on the recall ballot and then went on to win reelection in 2006.

Today, Schwarzenegger advocates for eating less meat, particularly in professional sports. He produced the documentary *The Game Changers* (with longtime pal James Cameron), which explores the rise in meat-free athletes. Throughout the years, he continues to reinvent himself.

THE WORK IS NEVER DONE

Reinvention requires reflection. Schwarzenegger reflected upon his life, decided he wanted to improve upon it, and made a change. Throughout the years, he has made these changes continuously.

Optimizing culture (the focus of Chapter 7) means establishing a control point and measuring the variance to ensure an upward trajectory toward an ideal culture state. Continuous cultural improvement means perpetual optimization—the work is never done.

> **Continuous Cultural Improvement:** *A robust and consistent company culture that drives ideal outcomes takes hard, deliberate work on a continuous basis. It requires all leaders to adopt and apply a strong understanding of values, from the shop floor to the C-suite.*

It's like adding a back deck or pool to your house. It doesn't optimize your house, like cleaning and maintaining it does, but it

---

17 "Bio," ArnoldSchwarzenegger.com, accessed July 8, 2021, http://schwarzenegger.com/bio.

improves it and increases its value. Continuous cultural improvement means evaluating the positive and negative outcomes of cultural performance over a consistent period of time to influence business decisions. It looks at shifts in an organization's control point and how to tweak behavioral expectations and standards for engagement to align with the company values. Continuous improvement means asking questions such as:

- How can I continue to amend the job descriptions for my floor supervisors to reflect the behavioral expectations that align with our culture?
- Should I change my recruitment strategy because I realize there are certain professional backgrounds and industries that don't perform our standards for engagement well?

Continuous cultural improvement is leveraging the visibility gained when you operationalize and then optimize your culture to better support your cultural performance future state. We aren't suggesting you change your values at this stage, but we *do* recommend you continue to review and evaluate them. You may find that a few need a little life breathed into them.

Continuous cultural improvement means keeping your optimal cultural state running as efficiently (and profitably) as possible. It means having cultural clairvoyance.

Cultural Clairvoyance: *The ability within leaders to assess the current cultural state and behavior and perceive future events and outcomes based on that assessment. The ability to perceive (predict and determine) the need for action before negative impacts occur. As it is, it will continue to be.*

When you have cultural clairvoyance you breathe culture—you can feel it and touch it. It's tangible. Optimizing is figuring out what doesn't work and then fixing it; continuous cultural improvement goes beyond that. It means constantly evaluating everything, like an internet of things (IoT) system that reviews efficiencies nonstop to figure out what is going to break *before* it does.

MICROCULTURES: BAD OR GOOD?

Evaluating everything, constantly, includes keeping a lookout for microcultures. Microcultures can be either negative or positive.

> **Microculture:** *Individual or siloed group cultures within an organization that may or may not be consistent with the desired company culture.*

Microculture is synonymous with subculture, and when one pops up in your organization, you could be in trouble, because detraction and division happen over time. No matter what you do, 20 percent of your leaders (your culture cogs) will slowly divert from the company's behavioral standards. This happens because of both internal and external forces, and when it does, microcultures are formed that detract from the culture control point.

Thanks to social learning, the behaviors of these microcultures are perpetuated throughout your organization. What makes them even worse is that in many cases, you won't even know they exist. Keeping a pulse on cultural engagement, via our CPM system, helps solve this problem. Without question, negative microcultures are a drag on *any* organization's culture and should be addressed.

But not all microcultures are negative—sometimes there are

microcultures holding the business up. These are the organization's cultural cheerleaders; they perpetuate the company's values and embody its acceptable behaviors.

Positive microcultures should be leveraged, not broken up, so we spend time identifying them during the assessment process. (Our *Cultural SWOT Analysis* and *Leader Behavioral DILOs* help us pinpoint who the cogs are and how they influence business outcomes.) We then determine how to integrate those microcultures into the system to contribute to the business and help scale it.

Some microcultures should be snuffed out and addressed, but others can be used to positively impact the organization's company culture.

CAN YOU AUDIT LEADERSHIP?

Fostering cultural improvement means practice and feedback (and identifying microcultures!), but to drive accountability, less guidance and coaching is needed—it's all about results and consequences, both positive and negative.

So, how are those results and consequences measured? Culture compliance.

> **Culture Compliance:** Set of supervisor and team audits designed to identify the degree of alignment to desired company culture, based upon specific measurable criteria.

Culture compliance is operational. Once culture performance management measurements are put in place, reviewing and assessing them quarterly or annually should be included in the organization's operational model.

Metrics like employee self-assessments and performance reviews, employee engagement scores, and cultural performance scores should all be included in a culture compliance audit. If indicators report that a leader is contributing to culture control point misalignment, a cultural performance improvement plan may be needed.

Culture compliance keeps everyone in check so that continuous cultural improvement is possible.

THE TRANSFORMATIONAL LEADER

Continuous culture improvement is much easier with the help of transformational leadership. Many of the most-engaged business leaders are beginning to acknowledge the urgent need to address their company culture. Internal and external socioeconomic and market pressures have prompted business leaders to acknowledge the impact their company culture has on their ability to attract and retain talent, achieve operational performance objectives, and appeal to market demands.

Business leaders have begun to realize their desired company culture is not reflected in the leadership behaviors and interactions that are observed daily. Thus their company culture has impacted how their frontline teams perform. This revelation has prompted business leaders to attempt to adopt a transformational company culture.

Most business leaders approach the concept of a transformational culture incorrectly and have minimized their business results as an outcome. A *transformational culture* is an effective workplace culture with key factors identified as staff empowerment, continuing development of practice, and self-knowledge. It is a culture that emphasizes self-energizing and self-organizing team members who have a clear sense of purpose, can communicate freely, challenge and support each other, take responsibility for innovation and development, and think critically about issues as they encounter them on a daily basis.[18]

Many business leaders attempt to transform their company culture while maintaining their current leadership style. Instead, only by transforming themselves and adopting a *transformational leadership approach* will true transformation occur throughout the culture of the organization, which will allow continuous improvement to happen.

Bernard Bass, industrial psychologist, defines transformational leadership with four critical components:[19]

- **Idealized Influence:** These leaders are purpose-driven role models who inspire and motivate followers to implement change. Their behavior is highly ethical. They are respected, trusted, and emulated by others.
- **Inspirational Motivation:** Leaders like these create inspirational visions that inspire exceptional performance—they have high standards and expectations, and are always optimistic. They motivate others to have a strong sense of purpose.
- **Intellectual Stimulation:** These leaders challenge assumptions and are risk-takers. When problem-solving, they collaborate with others and lobby for new ideas. They encourage critical thinking and autonomy.
- **Individualized Consideration:** Attending to unique needs, and serving others as a mentor, coach, or guide, is the role

18 Kim Manley, "Transformational Culture: A Culture of Effectiveness," *Practice Development in Nursing*, (August 2004), https://doi.org/10.1002/9780470698884.ch4.

19 Ibid.

of these leaders. They listen to concerns, are empathic, and provide support. They also recognize and help develop individualized talents.

These components are adopted by members of an organization who seek to foster change to achieve optimal business outcomes. Individuals who seek to foster commitment to change among subordinates do so by creating and communicating a vision that serves as inspiration and the catalyst for team mobilization—this is transformational leadership in action.[20]

Transformational leadership aligns with the principles of change management as both approaches emphasize the need to shift an organization's personnel, systems, and processes from the current state to the desired state by determining an organization's capability and capacity to change.[21] Therefore, most businesses require transformative leaders who can contribute to an organization's efforts to adapt, control, and affect change as it occurs.[22]

Business leaders seeking to transform their company culture must evaluate how they influence communication, change, and outcomes for their business.

INFLUENCING COMMUNICATION

Transformational leadership requires a leader's ability to influence individuals through passion and motivation, often a derivative

20 Kathy Cowan-Sahadath, "Business Transformation: Leadership, Integration, and Innovation—A Case Study," *International Journal of Project Management* 28, no. 4 (May 2010), https://doi.org/10.1016/j.ijproman.2009.12.005.

21 Craig Luzinski, "Transformational Leadership," *The Journal of Nursing Administration* 41, no. 12 (December 2011), https://doi: 10.1097/NNA.0b013e3182378a71.

22 V. Tamilarasu, "Change Management," *International Journal of Management Prudence* 4, no. 2 (2012), http://www.publishingindia.com/ijmp/19/change-management/184/1439/.

of a detailed vision that is captured with unique interpretations from subordinate stakeholders.[23] A transformational leader considers the importance of face-to-face interaction as a method of reciprocal communication.

Communication must be information-rich, with an emphasis on identifying verbal and nonverbal indicators that recipients clearly understand and are aligned and ready to execute on one's vision. This skill requires a measurable degree of cognitive and emotional intelligence.[24] A leader with emotional intelligence has a distinct ability to remain aware of one's emotions, with a strong capacity to control and express oneself with empathy.[25]

As most methods of communication adopt the use of technology, transformative leaders recognize the value of interpersonal communication between individuals to exercise one's emotional intelligence in a more diligent and effective manner. Furthermore, transformational leaders should nurture a workplace culture that encourages the development of fellow stakeholders' emotional intelligence through education, training, and feedback.

Ultimately, transformational leadership plans should include a commitment to maintaining an apparent level of transparency among stakeholders, thus contributing to a work environment that is focused on results, while avoiding lost time due to individuals trying to seek and understand the motive behind a leader's request or actions. Transparency in business requires transformational leaders to remain informative with subordinates about one's goals, including the historical trends, potential barriers, and

---

23 Luzinski, "Transformational Leadership."

24 Diane Henry, "Emotional Intelligence," *American Journal of Nursing* 117, no. 10 (October 2017), https://doi: 10.1097/01.NAJ.0000525856.75439.4a.

25 Ibid.

level of importance to the organization that may affect business outcomes.

INFLUENCING CHANGE

Aligning transformational leadership approaches to foster change, this method focuses on the influence one can have over individuals and social systems.[26] As a transformative leader, one must focus on driving inspiration among individuals and teams as the method to drive higher performance of subordinates. A transformational leader's cultural change strategy includes active considerations of the factors that drive the need for change and how one can proactively design and implement change management initiatives that appeal to an evolving workforce.

In today's social and economic climate, business leaders are faced with complex organizational challenges that are often a derivative of unanticipated changes in their workplace culture. These cultural changes are frequently a result of an inherent evolution of the workforce profile and demographic.

In recent years, the need for transformational leadership has been heightened by the generational gaps that exist between a "legacy'" workforce and recent new hires postured to drive the company forward. Baby boomer and Generation X employees are now working with millennial and Gen Z peers.[27]

---

26 Luzinski, "Transformational Leadership."

27 Raquel Escortell, Asier Baquero, Beatriz Delgado, "The Impact of Transformational Leadership on the Job Satisfaction of Internal Employees and Outsourced Workers," *Cogent Business and Management* 7, vol. 1 (October 2020), https://doi: 10.1080/1528008X.2015.1048920.

INFLUENCING OUTCOMES

Transformational leadership influences outcomes by adopting an approach with subordinates that expresses a genuine desire to identify a need for change and collaboration. This will help develop an aligned vision for desired outcomes.[28] Successful transformational company culture objectives are achieved when leaders recognize the impact that purposeful development and personal motivation can have on a workforce.[29] Transformational leaders understand and apply the principles of influence by relating to a worker's personal inspirations and connecting them to the outcomes one desires to achieve.

A transformational leader must work to drive teams to achieve a state of high performance, requiring workgroups to overcome the challenges associated with bringing independent thinkers together to achieve a common goal.

ADVANTAGES OF TRANSFORMATIONAL LEADERSHIP

While there are many factors that can be attributed to the advantages of a transformational leadership approach, one of the most critical advantages of this leadership style includes the ability to formulate a vision for growth and mobilize a group accordingly.[30]

Inspired by positive examples of present-day practitioners of leadership, many progressive business leaders aspire to adopt a transformational leadership approach like notable business pro-

---

28   Luzinski, "Transformational Leadership."

29   Ibid.

30   Ibid.

fessional, investor, and philanthropist Richard Branson. (If you recall, Kate Winslet rescued his mother from a house fire.)

Some of the key characteristics that describe Branson's leadership approach include "self-motivator, aggressive, risk-taker, financially organized, excellent negotiator, creative, flexible, very competitive, proactive, hardworking, and charismatic." These are all behaviors indicative of a transformative leadership style.[31]

Branson applied a naturally transformative approach to his leadership style, attributing his success to his ability to motivate and mobilize his team around him.

He shared his belief that maintaining a family-like organization with a strong team who all believe that "employees or associates come first, clients second, and shareholders third."

Branson believes that higher compensation is not the key motivator of his employees; on the contrary, he supports the notion that a good work environment, healthy work-life balance, and feeling appreciated and empowered are the principles of driving a successful team.

A leader's adoption of a transformational approach, seeking to engage, motivate, and empower others to act, will positively impact how one approaches a company culture transformation. Cultural transformation requires a workforce that is energized by the notion that the leadership team trusts one's ability to perform at a level that does not require constant oversight.

A strong advantage of transformational leadership is the level of

---

31 Ibid.

empowerment that is realized because of one's effort to achieve a state of high performance among workgroups. Transformational leaders establish a clear and concise mission, vision, and value statement, including the notion that these principles serve as the driving force behind the strategic decision-making practices in the organization, from talent acquisition to business development.[32]

DISADVANTAGES OF TRANSFORMATIONAL LEADERSHIP

Contrary to the success experienced by many business leaders because of one's focus on empowerment as a tool to drive performance outcomes, transformational leadership also has a few disadvantages. Transformational leaders often rely upon their ability to "paint" a clear and concise vision that teams can rally behind. Many business leaders have experienced business scenarios that included mobilization of workgroups that appeared to be aligned regarding project expectations. While the teams were motivated and reached a state of high performance, upon examination of results, there was a mismatch between the vision, objectives, and desired outcomes.

This misalignment was attributed to a lack of detail and transactional focus and oversight. Furthermore, transformational leadership approaches can rely too heavily on passion and emotion to influence change and outcomes, thus "clouding" the reality of the work environment.

For example, one may establish a vision for a team that includes each member's ability to execute with excellence on a very com-

32 Ana Čuić Tanković, "Defining Strategy Using Vision and Mission Statements of Croatian Organizations in Times of Crisis," *Economic Research* 26, vol. 1 (December 2013): 331–42, http://doi:10.1080/1331677X.2013.11517655.

plex process. It may also include the organization's ability to support the acquisition of resources in a timely manner to do so.

While one's passion and enthusiasm can successfully mobilize a team, one must not over-rely on this enthusiasm but rather invest in due diligence of research and reasoning to address potential barriers to success. Transformational leaders must be willing and able to share the reality of a situation and address how these circumstances may influence desired outcomes. These same principles apply to transforming a company culture.

LIVE AND BREATHE YOUR CULTURE

Cultural transformation is possible when leadership knows their culture so well they don't need to rehearse it. Their understanding of their culture is transformed. They understand the implications of a misaligned culture—it's the antithesis of predictability. When an organization's culture performance management score is high, senior executives can predict the areas of the business that will have the greatest impact.

From a lean management point of view (a production time reduction method used in manufacturing), the reference to continuous improvement speaks to the business leaders' ongoing effort to improve their products, services, or processes. These efforts can seek "incremental" improvement over time or "breakthrough" improvement all at once. In either case, whenever these products, services, or processes involve people to engage with or manage, human capital management strategies must be applied.

Culture performance management serves as a mechanism for continuous improvement, because it helps leaders improve how they interact with others and make decisions on behalf of the business.

CultureWorx provides a measurement for what many thought was intangible or difficult to understand. You can't improve what you can't accurately manage and measure—the platform solves for that.

That, combined with transformational leadership, will help ensure the long-term sustainability of the business. Transformational leadership leads to cultural confidence. It is an outcome of effective culture performance management.

> **Cultural Confidence:** *The degree to which an organization's leadership knows that the right behaviors, and stated values and goals, are truly implemented.*

Over time, when culture is evaluated, optimized, and continually improved, you can understand the changes and actions that truly influence your organization's performance. You know how far you can push your leadership team, and you know your decisions are rooted in integrity because they model the company's cultural behaviors and standards. You aren't worried about a culture audit because you're confident an assessment will reveal a cultural vision being executed and managed on a daily basis.

Culture confidence means less stress and anxiety around day-to-day behaviors, which improves productivity and positively impacts the organization's bottom line.

No matter which profession he chose to pursue, Schwarzenegger was confident. He knew how to optimize the rules of each game he played and continuously improved upon his life.

Company culture isn't something you can fix once and then walk away. It needs constant TLC. Continuous cultural improvement means the work is never done.

CASE STUDY: THE BROKEN CPM

A global manufacturer, innovator, and technical solutions provider for the automotive industry had selected and defined their values before they began working with us. They had gone through a recent acquisition that pushed them to reevaluate their values and use behavioral expectations to specifically define them—they attached defining and defeating behaviors that aligned with their values.

After that, though, their plan started to fall apart because they skipped the connection step and went straight to learn. They utilized traditional, classroom-style learning techniques (which were ineffective) and conducted employee pulse surveys (a lagging indicator) to measure their cultural heartbeat, and it was all ineffective.

Behavioral expectations must be tied to day-to-day work execution. Connection points must be established so leadership behavioral practice can be standardized and measured. Where are leaders practicing and exhibiting the behaviors? Do they live up to the culture we're trying to promote, standardize, and scale?

Our client knew the importance of standardizing and scaling culture, but they didn't know how to move from a definition to a connection point and create a practical approach to measurement, action, and development in real time.

They brought us on board because despite their efforts, they hadn't penetrated the frontline employees because they didn't know how to connect management operating points. We helped them establish a roadmap: the culture performance management system.

CHAPTER 16

ESG

THE FUTURE OF YOUR COMPANY CULTURE

Audit. The five-letter word that causes fear and panic for almost all of us.

The IRS is probably the most well-known for its tax audits—safety and ISO audits have been happening for decades. New to the scene are the social responsibility standards required to attain a social license to operate (SLO). An SLO includes human rights criteria regarding the labor force. Today, society expects organizations to stand by the culture they espouse—to talk the talk and walk the walk—and if they don't, there's a good chance Twitter is going to hear about it.

Coca-Cola takes this social responsibility seriously. So does Walmart. Each has supplier guiding principles (SGP) that determine the acceptable practices standards companies must adhere to in order to qualify to be a supplier. Both Coca-Cola and Walmart established criteria that suppliers must measure and demonstrate and are issuing SLOs that are grounded in a supplier's ability to understand and demonstrate their social and environmental stewardship.

This is all done so that Coca-Cola and Walmart can minimize and mitigate risks within their own organizations. To take it a step further, they've started to do random culture audits; they arrive at a supplier's manufacturing site, warehouse, or corporate office, unexpectedly, to see if the culture on the ground matches the culture on paper. If it doesn't, the supplier partnership will likely be terminated. A lack of standardized, operationalized, and optimized culture has the potential of costing the supplier millions.

Culture audits are becoming more and more mainstream and companies everywhere, across all industries, need to prepare for them.

ESG

We want you to have an honest, candid, and transparent look at your culture, to help you prepare for these culture audits. Examine your frontline leaders—do you think they have the capacity to acknowledge that cultural change is not only needed, but that *they* need to be leading the charge? Frontline leaders will play a pivotal role in the cultural change process, and if they don't have the right mindset, they won't be very effective. If they aren't effective, business sustainability could become a problem.

When you look at the marketplace through a lens of sustainability, more and more organizations are focusing on three main categories over the next five years: environmental, social, and governance, otherwise referred to as ESG.

1. **Environmental sustainability** has been in the forefront for the last fifteen years or so; the focus has shifted from resource depletion to deforestation and waste pollution.
2. **Social sustainability** is the number one topic of conversation

right now. Current discussions center on how social interest impacts economic stability—conversations about employee relations, diversity, equality, inclusion, and workplace conditions happen in the local community, as well as how each impacts the broader commerce spectrum.

3. **Governance sustainability** covers everything from taxation to political lobbying or affiliations to corruption. It's a wider look at the institution of diversity infrastructures.

Of all three, the current market is focusing primarily on social sustainability. Because social interests must now be applied to organizational constructs, businesses can no longer ignore how their actions impact employee relations and desired social norms. Institutions will be forced to measure their social impact from an internal workplace standpoint.

Working conditions, employee health, conflict resolution, and diversity have all become so critical that organizations must spend time focusing on them. In the past, minor cultural awareness was enough to pass in the marketplace. Most companies had a list of values and that was it. No one examined them or validated whether or not they were authentic and being applied in the workplace.

That laissez-faire attitude has shifted—now, you have to prove you live and breathe your values, otherwise there are massive organizations that won't partner with you as a supplier or vendor. Coca-Cola and Walmart are already moving in this direction, so how long do you think it will take before all major companies are, too?

Culture performance management enables businesses to mobilize around the social component of ESG, because it provides them with insight to focus on behaviors that align with their values and it gives them metrics to use for credibility. There is integrity to action when it is backed up by data; it's also easier to measure progress (or regression). Data makes a sustainable culture more plausible, because measurable metrics allow for continuous improvement.

CIRCLE OF SUSTAINABILITY

Sustainable culture requires a practice of continuous improvement. The Circle of Sustainability model helps us assess and understand sustainability toward sustainable, social outcomes. It enables us to better understand and predict sustainability and market dominance because it assesses ecology, economics, politics, and culture.

Circles of Sustainability

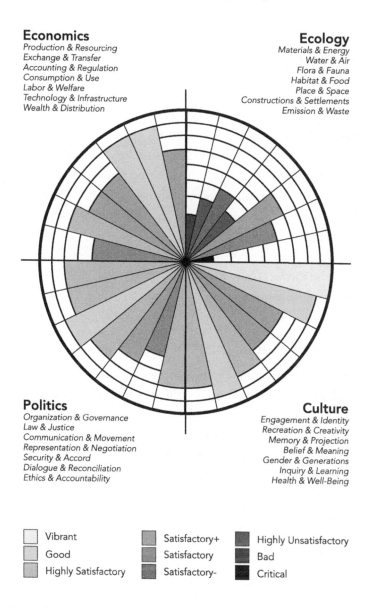

Economics
Production & Resourcing
Exchange & Transfer
Accounting & Regulation
Consumption & Use
Labor & Welfare
Technology & Infrastructure
Wealth & Distribution

Ecology
Materials & Energy
Water & Air
Flora & Fauna
Habitat & Food
Place & Space
Constructions & Settlements
Emission & Waste

Politics
Organization & Governance
Law & Justice
Communication & Movement
Representation & Negotiation
Security & Accord
Dialogue & Reconciliation
Ethics & Accountability

Culture
Engagement & Identity
Recreation & Creativity
Memory & Projection
Belief & Meaning
Gender & Generations
Inquiry & Learning
Health & Well-Being

Vibrant
Good
Highly Satisfactory

Satisfactory+
Satisfactory
Satisfactory-

Highly Unsatisfactory
Bad
Critical

In today's marketplace, the business emphasis is on manpower, culture, and the learning process. There was a time when the learning process was placed more on the political side of the circle (or the governance component of ESG) because sentient educational systems served as the driver of economic stability. Government-sanctioned institutions created an industrialized education model that fueled the industrial economy. It was a regimented curriculum that taught the basics.

Public schools are still in line with this model. There's a reason why they all follow certain cadences—when the bell rings to signal the end of recess, schoolchildren stop playing and run back to their classroom. This style of learning is meant to mobilize the masses educationally around what will support economic well-being.

Using the Circles of Sustainability model helps ensure continuous improvement for your company culture.

YOU CAN'T IGNORE CULTURE

Your culture doesn't have to be perfect—but it needs to be measured, managed, and tracked to ensure continuous improvement.

The emphasis has shifted from government constructs to a focus on the *social* constructs, especially culture. The workplace is changing—more than 50 percent of the working population are millennials—and social and cultural considerations are front and center.

Both ESG and the Circle of Sustainability show that organizations can't ignore culture—it is an integral part of any marketplace discussion for consumers, suppliers, *and* employers. Adopting a CPM system enables organizations to get in front of the curve.

Today, these are some of the questions consumers ask:

- What are your values?
- What is your mission statement?
- What is your belief process?

Culture performance management is how organizations can measure whether their social impact is healthy. Any business looking for an investment has to demonstrate its social impact. A positive EBITDA is no longer good enough. Without proof of a sustainable culture, acquiring funding will be a struggle.

IS YOUR CULTURE A FACADE?

Company culture has become a facade for many businesses and not a practice—that's one of the reasons these culture audits exist. When values are a vehicle for public relations or tools for marketing (instead of representative of how they honestly behave and interact with internal and external stakeholders), they usually cease to connect with the company's overarching operational growth and sustainability vision.

If leaders focus on outward appearances and conceal a less pleasant or creditable reality, they are putting on a facade, even as it relates to one's company culture. The most revealing facades are exposed by a leader's failed attempt at defining and communicating their company's values.

The most innovative leaders recognize that the pursuit of achieving operational excellence requires a strategic examination of *all* the components of one's business—they look beyond the systems and processes that support it.

But many business leaders cannot explain their company culture in the context of business impact or outcomes. When this happens, they have failed to operationalize their culture. They haven't connected a genuine value and belief system that drives positive business outcomes to a framework that demonstrates how individuals should behave and interact with one another.

Your company culture—as defined by the values system that exists within your organization, the consciousness that internal stakeholders have around that value system, and your leadership team's ability to exhibit and practice the behaviors that espouse those values—is the difference between realizing positive or negative outcomes for your business.

Is your culture a facade that will crumble when the media begins throwing rocks or is your culture a bulkhead prepared to sustain any assault?

Only by measuring and managing your culture via CPM can you truly know whether you stand behind a flimsy display or a strong defense.

YOUR COMPETITIVE ADVANTAGE

In the spring of 2021, Major League Baseball (MLB) pulled the All-Star Game out of Atlanta[33] in protest of an election bill signed by Georgia Governor Brian Kemp to change voting laws.[34]

The reality is everyone is becoming more socially conscious, including investors. They're measuring investment potential based on whether an organization meets specific social criteria. If the organization doesn't, it's unlikely they'll get the funds.

We aren't arguing for either side—we're simply using the example to show you the implications of today's social sensitivities and how they impact business. You can't ignore the social environment. Instead, you have to get in front of it using CPM, so that you have a construct around your culture that can prove you live and breathe it every day.

---

33 David K. Li, Jane C. Timm, and Adrianne Morales, "MLB Pulls All-Star Game from Atlanta in Protest of Restrictive New Voting Law," NBCNews.com, April 2, 2021, https://www.nbcnews.com/news/us-news/mlb-pulls-all-star-game-georgia-wake-restrictive-new-voting-n1262930.

34 "Georgia Gov. Kemp Signs GOP Election Bill Amid an Outcry," CNBC.com, March 26, 2021, https://www.cnbc.com/2021/03/26/georgia-gov-kemp-signs-gop-election-bill-amid-an-outcry.html.

PREPARE FOR THE "S"

Culture performance management is a competitive advantage because it prepares businesses for the S of ESG. Even financial companies like Goldman Sachs have it figured out. They're releasing annualized reports that review their ESG approaches, the impact on their bottom line, and the influence it has on their decision-making as a lender.[35]

ESG is trending, and if you aren't already considering its impact on your business, quite frankly you're behind. In today's world, you have to appeal to prospective consumers, suppliers, vendors, *and* financial investors—they're all going to hold you to a high social and cultural standard. Talent already does. CPM will keep your internal and external stakeholders happy, *and* it helps with retention because a healthy culture attracts top talent.

There are companies with entire teams dedicated to organizational leadership and culture initiatives. Their specific objective is to operationalize their culture in a way that's tangible, sustainable, and intimate. These teams are also responsible for ensuring standards are set for all prospective suppliers and vendors. They don't want anyone misrepresenting the business, because it could result in a $10 million sponsorship or investment loss.

Companies have to change their thinking and reimagine their culture—society is forcing it. A static model won't be able to keep up with the change and will fall behind. Cultural performance management is needed to help prepare you for the S of ESG. And considering what we're seeing from companies like MLB, if you aren't on board, you're already behind.

---

35   "The Future, Now: Integrating Sustainability with Purpose across Our Business," Goldman Sachs 2020 Sustainability Report, https://www.goldmansachs.com/s/sustainability-report/index.html.

From Culture to Culture was written to make you aware of alternative methods to measure and increase employee engagement (these days, that means thinking about what's going on socially) and introduce you to culture performance management. Its goal was to then show you how you can easily operationalize (CultureWorx), optimize, and set your company culture up for continuous improvement.

We established in Part 1 that You Can't Fake Company Culture, otherwise you're in a culture conundrum. Meaning, your days are numbered, because today's social criteria and standards have changed. Now, you have to epitomize the culture you claim to represent—you have to be culturally credible.

The CPM system was introduced in Part 2. Once you accept reality, you can start to operationalize it. In Part 2, we covered the seven pillars of the culture performance management system:

- Pillar #1: Select
- Pillar #2: Define
- Pillar #3: Learn
- Pillar #4: Connect
- Pillar #5: Practice
- Pillar #6: Measure
- Pillar #7: Refine

We also covered the assessments we use to evaluate each step. Before you can implement the CPM system, you have to assess your culture and identify the areas that need some work. What's your culture baseline and cultural capacity?

In Part 3, we showed you how CultureWorx can help operationalize culture performance management. Is it possible without our platform? Yes, but it will be tedious and take a while. The platform will help you:

- **Select** and **define** a value system
- Determine how to **connect** with it
- **Learn** and **practice** the behaviors associated with those values
- **Measure** their success when they **practice** the behaviors that align with the values
- **Refine** the values and behaviors for increased value

After operationalization comes optimization. Now that you're using CultureWorx and the CPM system is in place, how do you improve it? What behaviors and standards for engagement need improving? How do you establish a culture centerline, identify your culture cogs, and optimize your culture? (The platform can help with all of that, too.)

Cultural optimization leads to continuous culture improvement. You can't optimize once and walk away—if you do, all your hard work will fall apart. Continuous cultural improvement means cultural confidence, cultural clairvoyance, and perpetual cultural assessment. It also means incorporating it into recruiting and training programs.

Culture performance management is a competitive advantage.

A GUIDED PATH

It's unclear whether or not the state of Georgia was prepared for the MLB's course of action. Regardless, it happened, and the state lost revenue. It's critical for today's organizations to keep a close eye on the S of ESG, so they aren't caught off guard (and lose millions in tax revenue the state would have seen from purchases at the event).

CPM defines acceptable behaviors and standards for engagement to ensure employees act consistently. It also measures these behaviors and provides data to prove claims are supported by action. Otherwise, it's your word against someone else's. If a false claim is made about your culture, you can prove them wrong because you proactively measure and manage it.

As we mentioned at the very beginning of the book, the information within has been laid out sequentially for a reason. Each part of the book and step in the CPM system builds on itself, like a house. The foundation is laid before the frame. If you frame the house first, it won't be sturdy enough to hold the weight.

Culture performance management is no different. The system is built from the bottom up via a simple, yet prescribed, step-by-step process. If the user goes off track and skips ahead to *Practice* after values and behaviors have been selected and defined, their efforts are destined to go awry. These days, it's easy to veer off course because there are so many distractions in the world. The CPM system provides you with a guided path that's easy to follow.

If at any point along the way you have questions or are confused about which way to go, give us a call. We're an open door and happy to continue the dialogue. We'll answer any questions you have, and we also love a challenge. Talking culture is what we do, and if you disagree with us, we welcome that conversation, too.

So, test our theories and ask your employees, prospective employees, and clients how important company culture is to them. Ask your vendors and suppliers, too.

Culture has always been the key to sustained business success, but in today's marketplace, it's critical. Now, organizations have

the tool to measure and manage it—our culture performance
management system.

PART 4

APPENDICES

APPENDIX A

———

GLOSSARY

Company Culture: *The values we share, the language we use, the behaviors we display, and the connections we have with others. The values set the standard for how individuals must engage and interact. The definition of the values determines the behaviors individuals must exhibit within a company culture. The shared understanding of the definition of these values and behaviors establishes the common language used within a company culture. The practice of these behaviors establishes how individuals engage and interact within a company culture.*

Continuous Cultural Improvement: *A robust and consistent company culture that drives ideal outcomes takes hard, deliberate work on a continuous basis. It requires all leaders to adopt and apply a strong understanding of values, from the shop floor to the C-suite.*

Cultural Baseline: *Established behavioral strengths and weaknesses metrics from which you can train, evaluate, monitor, and improve the behaviors and attitudes of executive management and frontline leaders.*

Cultural Cadence: *The rhythmic pattern of a company's culture—a* *pattern that allows teams to know what they are doing and when it will occur. The purpose of a cadence is to establish a reliable and dependable cultural capability that demonstrates a predictable capacity.*

Cultural Capacity: *The specific ability of an organization or resource to consistently attain a degree of excellence in demonstrating the ideal set of management and the frontline leader behaviors required to achieve 100 percent attainment of operational capacity.*

Culture Centerline: *Pulling from statistical process control, a culture centerline is the control point for measuring and tracking variation in cultural performance management. Deviations from the centerline indicate variability in behavior, which drives organizational company culture. Variability/deviation too far from the centerline triggers leadership that something has shifted in attitude, belief, or behavior and should be examined, understood, and addressed.*

Cultural Chaos: *When a company has a set of values but hasn't standardized the definitions of those values, acceptable behavior cannot be established and taught. The result is behavioral disarray and bedlam.*

Cultural Character: *The "personality"/nature/temperament of a company's culture—the state of the stakeholder's mindset (attitudes and behaviors) as reflected within the work environment.*

Cultural Clairvoyance: *The ability within leaders to assess the current cultural state and behavior and perceive future events and outcomes based on that assessment. The ability to perceive (predict and determine) the need for action before negative impacts occur. As it is, it will continue to be.*

Cultural Climate: *The current "temperature" of organizational* company culture at any given time assessed. It's how the workplace environment impacts the culture. Not the vision or the perception—it's what's actually happening.

Culture Cog: *The individual within an organization represents the primary driver of an outcome. In the case of CPM, they are frontline supervisors who drive appropriate behaviors, down to team members in support of desired company culture and operational efficiency. These individuals keep the wheels of an organization turning and in alignment.*

Culture Compass: *The method and tool that allows managers to frequently ensure their cultural interactions behaviors are in sync with the cultural requirements.*

Cultural Competence: *The degree to which an organization successfully and efficiently manages and consistently exhibits and drives behavior toward its ideal cultural state—an organization's ability to consistently and effectively manifest the behaviors that exemplify its company culture.*

Culture Compliance: *Set of supervisor and team audits designed to identify the degree of alignment to desired company culture, based upon specific measurable criteria.*

Cultural Confidence: *The degree to which an organization's leadership knows that the right behaviors, and stated values and goals, are truly implemented.*

Cultural Connections: *Where and when defined leadership behaviors must be practiced during the daily execution of work.*

Cultural Consciousness: *The state of being awake and aware of one's* *organizational culture, emphasizing the values that shape the behaviors and interactions between individuals within an organization.*

Cultural Constraint: *The discrepancy between your ideal company culture and its current state, which results in negative behavioral impacts on morale, productivity, efficiency, and overall engagement. Most organizations are culturally constrained—they want to realize their ideal cultural state but don't have effective tools to do so.*

Culture Control Point: *Frontline leaders demonstrate value-based behaviors in action. This is the group of people to be developed and managed in order to effectively demonstrate and execute the company culture you desire. They can have the greatest positive cultural impact on your employees.*

Culture Conundrum: *Having an organizational company culture contrary to what is desired by executive leadership—wishing for one type of company culture but having somehow ended up with another.*

Cultural Corruption: *An unaligned workforce resulting in negative impacts on morale, productivity, efficiency, and overall organizational interactions that are based upon behaviors, exhibited by company leaders, and are misrepresentative of the ideal company culture.*

Cultural Credibility: *The degree to which an organization lives up to its desired company culture as perceived by its relationship to people, both internally (employees) and externally (clients, media, etc.).*

Culture Crux: *The core issues underlying a company culture—an essential point requiring problem identification and behavioral resolution.*

Cultural Engagement: *A single-number metric used to measure how* *engaged the individuals within an organization are in its desired company culture. Typically, a post-metric.*

Culture Performance Management (CPM): *Culture performance management refers to the system for aligning an organization's core company values with specific and actionable leadership behaviors that can be practiced, evaluated, and measured in real time in order to drive immediate improvement in how leaders engage, interact, and make decisions. The ultimate objective is to foster short-interval and continuous improvement of one's company culture. This is achieved through the implementation of a comprehensive CPM that connects leadership engagement and work execution touchpoints that ultimately influence business performance outcomes. CPM is designed to support the sustainability of performance results. It also provides visibility into the progress leaders make toward practicing the behaviors that serve as an ideal company culture requisite.*

Core Score: *A defined set of metrics reported daily and/or weekly that demonstrates the degree to which frontline supervisors and managers are demonstrating and driving actions and behaviors in support of an organization's desired company culture.*

Core Workout: *The management process of actively comparing self-evaluation of real-time behaviors to the cultural ideal to a manager's evaluation of the same behaviors, and then engaging in active discussion and development to move these behaviors closer to the ideal.*

Microculture: *Individual or siloed group cultures within an organization that may or may not be consistent with the desired company culture.*

Strategic Learning Environment: *A specifically orchestrated systematic series of developmental activities (including engagement sessions,* *forum boards, knowledge testing, and practicum) designed to develop superior frontline leadership behaviors to support a focused, aligned, and accountable leader for your organization.*

COMPANY CULTURE ASSESSMENTS

CULTURAL SWOT ANALYSIS

- **Definition:** Analysis of the strengths, weaknesses, opportunities, and threats facing the company that directly influence the leadership culture and performance outcomes.
- **Objective:** Leverage strengths, mitigate weaknesses, capitalize on opportunities, and minimize threats to the desired leadership culture.

CULTURAL VISION ALIGNMENT

- **Definition:** A qualitative and quantitative diagnostic tool that examines the perspectives of an organization's senior leaders to determine how they perceive the company culture, as compared to the ideal-state culture.
- **Objective:** To understand if the current-state vision and supporting practices surrounding the operational culture align with senior organizational leaders' desired ideal future-state company culture, identify disconnects in vision and practice, and reveal opportunities for better communication and clarity around cultural vision.

GOALS AND STRATEGIES ALIGNMENT

- **Definition:** A quantitative diagnostic tool designed to measure the organization's alignment between front-line leaders and their senior leadership team regarding the goals and the strategies required to meet organizational performance objectives.
- **Objective:** To reveal the adequacy and efficacy of top-down communication throughout the organization.

LEADERSHIP ATTITUDES AND BEHAVIORS (LAB) STUDY

- **Definition:** A qualitative and quantitative diagnostic tool designed to measure the level of awareness and comprehension of the distinct leadership skills and behaviors critical to driving positive operational performance outcomes that also align with an organization's cultural vision.
- **Objective:** To provide insight into the skills and behavioral development opportunities among leaders and measure and validate the level of alignment to the desired company culture expressed by leaders.

CULTURE DISCOVERY INTERVIEWS AND CONNECTION MAPPING

- **Definition:** A qualitative diagnostic used to solicit perspectives and insights from leaders regarding the factors that contribute to their ability to reach an optimal level of engagement, interaction, and decision-making.
- **Objective:** Foster trust and transparency among leaders by encouraging open and honest reflection on the barriers they encounter when attempting to engage and interact with employees, pinpoint the factors that positive or negative influence how leaders engage with employees and make decisions, and identify

the critical Cultural Connections during the execution of work where interactions occur between internal stakeholders.

LEADERSHIP SKILLS DEVELOPMENT SYSTEM CRITIQUE

- **Definition:** A qualitative and quantitative assessment of optimized learning and systems elements typically found in a world-class organization that supports the training and development of leaders.

- **Objective:** To identify the gaps within the current learning system that need to be filled, upgraded, or better utilized to improve its effectiveness and ensure the appropriate tools and resources are in place to support and reinforce front-line leadership team learning objectives; i.e. development resources, tools, materials, etc.

LEADER BEHAVIORAL DILO "DAY IN THE LIFE OF"

- **Definition:** An observational, qualitative diagnostic study used to identify what, when, and where leaders impact the business through their level of engagement and interaction in the work environment and how their behaviors are perpetuated in "real time."

- **Objective:** To examine and evaluate opportunities related to leadership engagement and decision-making, and to observe whether interactions and behaviors align with cultural performance expectations.

CULTURE PERFORMANCE MANAGEMENT SYSTEM EFFECTIVENESS CRITIQUE

- **Definition:** An assessment of elements we typically find in a world-class organization to support management of the leadership culture and associate processes.

- **Objective:** To determine opportunities within the current system that need to be upgraded or have better utilization.

COMMUNICATION EFFECTIVENESS STUDY

- **Definition:** Series of criteria, based on empirical observations, that use qualitative and quantitative data collection methods to check behavioral alignment and how employees are treated.
- **Objective:** To examine how leaders communicate with employees and each other and the tools used to facilitate communication.

ACKNOWLEDGMENTS

DR. DONTE VAUGHN, DM

I would like to thank my coauthor, Randall Powers, who has been a phenomenal visionary, collaborator, friend, and colleague. Your wisdom, insights, and leadership enabled our vision to become a reality.

I also want to acknowledge our entire Scribe team, especially Lisa Caskey, for her guidance, support, and contributions. You helped us embrace the personal and professional discipline and rigor required to author this book. You also fostered an exciting and fulfilling experience!

Finally, I give special thanks to our business partner, Sean Hart, and the countless others who supported us through this process. From our client-partners to the colleagues, family, and friends who encouraged us along the way, I thank you all!

RANDALL POWERS

I want to acknowledge my longtime business partner Sean Hart.

There are years between us in age; however, you are plenty of years wiser than me in many respects. Our style and talents are different, and yours have helped me fashion this CPM methodology to speak to the marketplace of today and now.

Dr. Donte Vaughn, my creative soulmate, what can I say? Thank you for the CPM construct and building a scientifically rooted, learning-focused, and results-based methodology that is well articulated, logically sound, and easy to facilitate with our client-partners. You are the blessing I needed, right when I needed it, and carried the relay baton across the finish line. What a brother and friend!

Shout-out to our entire team at CultureWorx and POWERS, who have given me feedback and shared their ideas on how to continuously improve our CPM methodology. Iron sharpens iron, always and respectfully.

I want to thank my mentor, Stan Stafford, a man of impeccable character and talent. You believed in me as a young man, and I carried you as my ideal as I became my own man.

Many thanks to Lisa Caskey from Scribe. Your ability to corral our wild and unbridled thoughts and ideas was nothing short of miraculous. Well done! I hope in some small way we return to you a new perspective on the "source" for a life with true meaning and purpose.

Lastly, and most importantly, I say a prayer of thanks!

ABOUT THE AUTHORS

DR. DONTE VAUGHN, DM

Dr. Donte Vaughn, DM, is an expert in organizational leadership, workforce management, and company culture, serving as a senior-level executive and business strategist for companies throughout the US and abroad. He has more than seventeen years of experience driving results in the public and private business sectors, fostering the design and implementation of business growth and leadership strategies. He currently holds two positions: chief culture officer and managing partner at CultureWorx, a culture performance management software and solutions company; and VP of organizational leadership and culture at POWERS, a cultural and operational performance management consulting firm. Before working with CultureWorx and POWERS, Dr. Vaughn founded and managed a boutique operational management consulting practice serving the small business community. He also performed at a senior executive capacity for firms providing labor strategy and workforce management solutions for the industrial market space.

Dr. Vaughn studied at Drexel University and the University of

Phoenix, where he received a bachelor's degree in business administration and management and a master's degree in management/organizational leadership. He also has the honor and distinction to serve as a doctor of management, concentrating in organizational leadership and culture. His professional memberships include the Society for Human Resource Management (SHRM), National Speakers Association (NSA), National Small Business Association's Leadership Council, and the National Business Educators Association (NBEA).

RANDALL POWERS

Randall serves as a managing partner for both CultureWorx and POWERS. He concentrates on product and new partnership development. He grew up in Augusta, Georgia, then moved to New Orleans to work as a tugboat deckhand for a year to earn money for college. Once enrolled at the University of Georgia (UGA), he loaded trucks at UPS, cutting his teeth as a frontline leader. Randall also met his beautiful wife, Beth, during his last semester at UGA. He holds a bachelor's degree in economics and philosophy and a master's degree in communications.

After graduate school and after leaving UPS, Randall entered the world of operational improvement where he learned the fundamentals of facilitating frontline leaders—to use skills and tools to optimize skills, processes, and performance. During this time, Randall also learned how to be a father to three awesome kids: Katey, Paul, and Ty. After ten years, Randall stepped away from his role as chief of operations to take the reins at Wise Metals group as president and COO.

A handful of years later, Randall started POWERS, a "boots on the ground" facilitation firm focused on delivering significant financial and operational value creation with its partners by optimizing culture and performance. Since 2009, POWERS has been optimizing performance by optimizing people for large and small companies across many different industries. Randall is also a founding member of CultureWorx (2020), a technology company that enables organizations to proactively develop, implement, measure, and improve the leadership skills, behaviors, interactions, and connections needed in real time to optimize employee engagement, inclusion, and equity.

Randall enjoys laughing with his witty wife, keeping his "dad bod" in somewhat good shape, and investing quality time developing the young adults in his businesses to understand and learn the real meaning and purpose of a life well lived.